The Poems Of John Byrom, Volume 3...

John Byrom, Chetham Society

REMAINS
Historical and Literary

CONNECTED WITH THE PALATINE COUNTIES OF

Lancaster and Chester.

VOLUME 70—NEW SERIES.

MANCHESTER:
Printed for the Chetham Society.
1912

The Chetham Society.

COUNCIL FOR 1911-12.

THE

𝔓oems

OF

JOHN BYROM.

EDITED BY

ADOLPHUS WILLIAM WARD,

P.B.A., Litt.D., Hon. LL.D., Hon. Ph.D.

Master of Peterhouse, Cambridge;   President of the Chetham Society.

VOL. III.

WITH AN APPENDIX OF UNPUBLISHED LETTERS
BY AND TO BYROM

PRINTED FOR THE CHETHAM SOCIETY.
1912.

PRINTED BY SHERRATT AND HUGHES
MANCHESTER AND LONDON

CONTENTS.

Contents

PREFACE.

IN bringing out this third, or supplementary, volume of the *Poems of John Byrom*, of which Volumes I and II were printed by the Chetham Society so far back as the years 1894 and 1895 respectively, I am tardily performing a duty towards a Society indulgent in no ordinary degree to its most unworthy President, as well as a slight labour of love for Byrom's native town. These additional pieces represent little more than the last fragments of his poetic productivity; but they comprise much that is characteristic of him—not only, in the way of verse, illustrating a delightful couplet to be found in the present volume:

" When a Man's in a Humour too Merry for Prose,
  His Words will be dancing in Spite of his Nose; "—

but also recalling his serious and solemn moods of thought. More and more, as he grew older, Byrom's high moral sense and deep religious feeling led him, not to despise forms, ecclesiastical or other, but to resist any tendency to overrate their value, while he was always prepared to welcome the spirit of Christianity even when divested of them. That, on occasion, his personal predilections—and prejudices—asserted themselves, by the side of these profounder emotions, was due to an element of humanity of which he did not think it necessary to feel ashamed. Here and there, the prolixity of advancing years becomes rather marked in these verses—a few being obviously written to order, so that the writer was fain, as he says,

" To patch 'em and piece 'em and turn 'em about,"

in order to comply with the wishes of good-natured friends. Elsewhere, he seems urged on by a desire of producing a complete century of lines—for what reason, he knew best. But, taking his verse for all in all, it displays the lasting freshness as well as simplicity of his mind—both qualities of true genius and often accompaniments of true scholarship.

In determining the order of sequence of the poems here printed, I have done my best to arrange them according to subject as well as (when this was feasible) chronologically. The imperfections of the result, will, I daresay, be excused in the case of so miscellaneous a collection.

In the *Table of Contents* of the present volume, the letters attached to the title of each piece there printed, indicate its single or double *provenance*. Variants have not been noted unless in exceptional instances.

The main body of the contents of the present volume are to be found in two MS. books in Chetham's Library, where they are marked respectively A—5—8 and Raines MSS. (MSS. bequeathed by the late Canon Raines) XLV. Two poems are contained respectively in the MSS. marked A—5—10 and Raines MSS. XXXIV.

A—5—8 (referred to as A in the present volume is a small quarto of 164 pages, and its contents form Part I of *A Miscellaneous Collection of Latin and English Poetry, chiefly Original*. A—5—10 (referred to here as B) forms Part III of the same collection. It bears the bookplate (modern) of Richard Baldwin; and the MS. is written in a very clear and well-formed hand. The first fourteen pieces in Volume I, together with No. 16, are stated in the Table of Contents to be "by Dr. Byrom." (No. 15 is the Rev. Thomas Cattell's *Answer* to Byrom's *Advice to the Rev. Messrs. H . . . . . and H . . . . . to Preach Slow*, for which see Volume I of the present edition. It begins:

"Brethren, as now I write in haste,
So I would have you to preach fast;")

but, as it has already been printed in Part II of Canon Raines' *Fellows of the Collegiate Church of Manchester* (edited by Dr. F. Renaud), pp. 230-2, there was no reason for reprinting it here. I cannot believe, with my distinguished predecessor, the late Mr. Crossley, that these lines were probably by Byrom himself. Of the other fifteen pieces, three have already been printed in the present edition, viz.: the epistle *To Henry Wright of Mobberley, Esq., on buying the Picture of Father Malebranche at a Sale* (Vol. I, pp. 77 *sqq.*); the epistle *To the Same* (the Rev. Messrs. H[addon] and H[eywood]) (*ib.*, M. 90 *sqq.*) and the epigram *A Lady's Love* (*ib.*, p. 210). I have also omitted *Verses designed for a Watchcase, applied to Shorthand*, an imitation of the verses printed in Vol. I, p. 571, of the present edition; since, though this piece is assigned to Byrom on the title-page of the *Collection*, I cannot conceive that he would have parodied his own fine lines. I have further taken the liberty of omitting the rather feeble epigram *On James's Powder* which has been ascribed to Byrom, but is not so ascribed in this MS. Of the remaining fifty pieces in the *Collection*, which include a series of verses, in Latin and in English, spoken by boys at the Manchester Grammar School *encaenia*, none is assigned to Byrom in the Table of Contents, and there seems no reason for supposing that any of them are his.

A—V—9 (here called B) contains the poem printed in the present volume under the title *On William III's horse Sorrel*, which in the table of contents of the MS. is ascribed to Byrom.

Vol. XXXIV of the Raines MSS. (here called C) contains, among much matter of interest, especially as to Jacobite affairs in the year 1745, the lines *On the Thanksgiving Day* printed in the present volume, with the accompanying letter.

Vol. XLV of the Raines MSS. (here called D) contains, together with most of the pieces included in A, a number of others—the majority copied in Canon Raines' neat and scholarly hand.   MS. D also contains copies of the following poems already printed in the present edition, viz.:

Postscript and part of body of *A Letter to R. L. Esq., on his Departure from London*, dated May 27th, 1725.   See Vol. I, pp. 38–46.

Verses on the Danger and Impropriety of Hastily Attaching Wrong Ideas to Words or Epithels.   See *ib.*, pp. 156–160.

The Ape and the Fox.   See *ib.*, pp. 160–162.

A Lady's Love.   See *ib.*, p. 219.

Verses on the Attack upon Admiral Byng in the "Monitor." See *ib.*, pp. 429–435.

Remarks upon Dr. Akenside's and Mr. Whitehead's Verses. See *ib.*, pp. 459–464.

Socrates' Reply concerning Heraclitus' Writings.   See Vol. II, pp. 333–338.

A plain Account of the Nature and Design of True Religoin. See *ib.*, pp. 374–376.

On the Nature and Reason of All Outward Law.   See Vol. II, pp. 413–415.

Of the Fall of Man.   [Part I.]   See *ib.*, pp. 520–523.

Part II of the last-named poem is printed from D, in the present volume.   I may take this opportunity of saying that I have ventured to ignore the possibility (for it cannot be said to be more than this) of the *Verses to a Friend who gave the Author a list of Shakespeare's Works*, (by the Rev. John Haddon), found by Mr. Axon among the Byrom Papers, having been written by Byrom.

Transcripts of the verses in A, B, C, and D were placed at my disposal, when I first undertook the editing of the present supplemental volume, through the kindness of Mr. W. E. A. Axon, by whom the originals were discovered in the course of his researches in Chetham's Library; but these transcripts have been carefully collated with the MSS. in the Library, the Feoffees of which most liberally permitted me to borrow the volume required.

The Feoffees, at the suggestion of Mr. C. W. Sutton, have also kindly allowed me to print, as an Appendix to the present volume some interesting letters by Byrom, which place it beyond doubt that he was the author of *An Account of Dr. Bentley's Case*. These letters, which were to have been edited for publication by the late John Eglington Bailey, were at one time supposed to have been lost (see *Introduction* to vol. i, p. iii, of this edition of Byrom's poems), but were rediscovered by Mr. Axon, to whom my volume is thus under a twofold debt. (See for an account of this rediscovery, the *Manchester Guardian* of April 10, 1903.)

In printing the verses contained in this volume, I have, in accordance with the principle adopted in the case of the earlier volumes—preserved the spelling of the MSS. (except where it is unintelligible or inconsistent with itself), including, so far as possible, the use of capital letters. The punctuation it seemed impossible to preserve; but I have tried to avoid unnecessary alterations.

In issuing this belated volume, I am conscious of many defects in what must perforce be its final form, and, more especially, of the too frequent recurrence of the word 'undiscoverable.' The instances would have been fewer, had the periodical literature of the day been better preserved in Manchester, in times when there was no Free Library and when the futile notion probably prevailed that it is useless to keep old newspapers.

It only remains to thank many friends and fellow lovers of Byrom for the aid they have given me without stint in the production of these pages—more especially the Hon. Secretary of our Society, Mr. C. W. Sutton, Chief Librarian of the Manchester Free Libraries, to whom I am indebted for constant and ready aid without which this volume could never have seen the light; Dr. W. E. A. Axon, who has largely supplemented my annotator's work from the resources of his antiquarian knowledge; Dr. Norman Moore, F.R.C.P.; Mr. J. L. Paton, High Master of the Manchester Grammar School;

the, Rev. Dr. W. E. Barnes, Fellow of Peterhouse and Hulsean Professor of Divinity in the University of Cambridge; Mr. I. Abrahams, Reader in Talmudic in the same University; Mr. J. A. Venn, of Trinity College, Mr. H. B. Wheatley, F.S.A., and Mr. A. T. Bartholomew, of Peterhouse and the Cambridge University Library, who has given me constant help, and whose Bentley bibliography has been of much use in connexion with my First Appendix.

Since the body of this volume was in print I have had the pleasure of reading Mr. Henry Broxap's *A Biography of Thomas Deacon, the Manchester Non-Juror.* (Publications of the University of Manchester; Manchester, 1911.) Mr. Broxap's book, which furnishes a full bibliography of Deacon's printed works, is a valuable contribution to the history of the Non-Jurors and to that of Manchester in the earlier half of the eighteenth century, and forms a notable tribute to the memory of a high-minded follower of a lost cause. Deacon, like his life long friend and constant correspondent Byrom, was by profession a physician, though he seems to have held no medical degree. The date of his consecration as Bishop would appear to have been 1734, or perhaps the previous year. To Mr. Broxap's book I owe one or two additions to the notes in the present volume.

A. W. W.

PETERHOUSE,
   CAMBRIDGE,
     June, 1912.

The Poems of John Byrom.

A PASTORAL BALLAD.

[This pleasant and refined example of the modernisation of a kind of dialogue which dates back to the *Clericus et Puella* of the thirteenth (or fourteenth) century, is worthy of the author of *My Time, O' ye Muses*. I have, therefore, given it precedence in the present batch of verses, so as to let it correspond to the famous *Pastoral* in vol. i, pp. 1 *sqq., ante.* The 'well said, loving Swain' of l. 27 is equally characteristic of the author's simple and courageous morality.]

WELL met, pretty Nymph,' said a jolly young Swain
　　To a beautiful Damsel acrossing the Plain;
' Why so much in haste?' (now the Month it was May)
' May I venture to ask you, fair Maiden, which way?'

To his Question the Nymph did straitway reply,
With a Smile on her Cheek and a Leer in her Eye:
" I came from yon' Village, and homeward I go;
And now, gentle Shepherd, pray, why would you know?"

' Fair Maiden, I hope you won't take it amiss,
If I tell you my Reason for asking you this:　　　　　10
I would see you safe home' (now the Swain was in love)
' Of such a Companion if you cou'd approve.'

" Your offer, kind Shepherd, is civil, I own;
But I see no great Danger in going alone;
Nor yet can I hinder, the way being free
To one as another, to you as to me."

B

' No danger in going alone, it is true;
But yet a Companion is pleasanter too;
And if you cou'd like' (now the Swain he took heart)
' Such a one as me, Mistress, we never shou'd part.'   20

"Oh! that's a long word," said the Shepherdess then;
" But I've often heard say, there's no minding you Men;
You'll say and unsay, you'll flatter and woo;
Then, leave a young Maiden's the first thing you do."

' O judge not so harshly!' the Shepherd reply'd;
' To prove what I say, I'll make thee my Bride;
To-morrow the Parson' (well said, loving Swain!)
' Shall join both our hands, and make one of us twain.'

Now, what the Nymph answer'd to this, is not said;
But, the very next day, to be sure they were wed.   30
Sing High diddle, ho diddle, high diddle down;
O when shall we have such a wedding in Town!

AN INVITATION TO BREAKFAST.

In Imitation of Philips' Style.

Addressed to R. Leycester, Esq.

[With these lines should be compared *A Letter to R. L., Esq., ante,* vol. i, pp. 30-1; also, the verses bearing the same title, *ib.,* pp. 38-46, both of which pieces clearly belong to the same period in the lives of Byrom and his intimate friend Ralph Leycester (alias 'Sir Peter') as that of the present effusion; the *Invitation,* like the earlier of the two *Letters,* alludes in a friendly way to 'Sir Peter's' love of the opera. That the present lines were written from Manchester, where both the friends must have been at the time when the one invited the other to breakfast, would seem to follow from the mention of the tavern patronised by them. Thus, we may date them in, or soon after, 1725, when Ralph Leycester had 'departed from London' for the country.

This is further suggested by the 'addition' stating that the verses are 'in imitation of Philips' style.' Byrom obviously had in mind Ambrose ('Namby-Pamby') Philips' tribute to the enchanting 'Rodelind' (the Cuzzoni), for which see *ante,* vol. i, p. 31. For it is clearly not the *Pastorals,* or the *Epistles to the Earl of Dorset,* that suggested Byrom's 'imitation,' but the lines to Cuzzoni, and possibly certain of the *Odes* addressed by Ambrose Philips to some very young ladies, Miss Margaret Pulteney and others, to which he owed the long-lived nickname first applied to him by Henry Carey. For the rest, the imitation is by no means close or otherwise striking. John Philips, the author of *Cyder,* who in his published poems confined himself to blank verse, is of course not in question.]

DEAR Sir Peter,
                          If these Numbers
Should surprize vou in your Slumbers;
If the drowsy God of Rest
Still detain you in your Nest;
If the Steams of Cookson's ale
Still in dainty Dreams exhale;
If the fairy-finger'd Francis
On your Brain-pan write Romances;
If, Sir Peter, this the Case is,
Prithee make no angry faces;   10
Make no bustle or bravado;
But, without any more ádo,
Come to Breakfast, Peter, pray do!

    And, if it be not too much labour,
First, O first awake thy Neighbour;
Lend his Nose a gentle tweak,
Or his Ears an Op'ra Squeak,
Or his formost Shins a Rub,
Or his ample front a Scrub,
Or his martial Sides a Thump,   20
Or a gen'rous Kick on's Rump,
Or whatever else may make him
To his Breeches to betake him!

7. Flowery-finger'd.—D.

15 Your Neighbour.—D.

1. Cf. Introduction, *ante.*

5. Cf. *To Mrs. Phebe Byrom,* l. 21, *post.* Jim Cookson was the landlord of 'The Spread Eagle' in Hanging Ditch, Manchester, at a later date the 'house of call' of politicians of very different tenets from those of Cookson's patrons. Cf. *Remains,* vol. i, pt. i, p. 313 and *note.*

7. Cf. *To Mrs. Phebe Byrom,* l. 23, *post.* Is this the 'profound F. Da[venpor]t,' mentioned as a whig consumer, rather than as a seller, of liquor, *Remains,* vol. i, pt. i, p. 29 *note*?

Now, for your drinking and your eating,
'Zooks! what nicetys are waiting:
Many a slice of bread and butt',
Thin as thinnest Wafers cut;
And the brownly-butter'd toast,
Crust or Crumb, which likes you most;
Rowl, or Manchet, white or brown—   30
Sure, they'll some of 'em go down!
But, if not, behold a dish,
Such as Gods themselves might wish;
Picklets, plump, and fresh, and round—
Mouths may water at the sound
Which to make, the jaws are able,
In a moment navigable!
But, if the last night's Enjoyment
Give your Jaws another time on't,
And your Entrails, what with Smoaking,   40
Laughing, Punning, Rhyming, Joking,
Be so dry, you know not whether
What you spit be froth, or feather—
Come, however, and with miscel-
-laneous liquor wet your Whistle:
Coffee, Tea, and Chocolate:
What a Deuce wou'd you be at?

30. *Manchet*: a loaf of fine bread.

34. *Picklet* is stated in *The Oxford Dictionary* to be 'an obsolete variant of pikelet (shortened from barapikelet), a Western and Midland name for a small round tea-cake, made of fine flour: a crumpet, or, in some districts, a muffin.' The name is still in use in Lancashire.

TO MRS. PHEBE BYROM.

[This epistle in verse from Byrom to his favourite sister forms a delightful *pendant* to his charming letters to her in the *Remains*. The keeping of Lent was not, so far as it would appear, one of the 'usages' as to the revival of which a dispute was long carried on among the Non-jurors, from the publication in 1717 of Jeremy Collier's first tractate on the subject onwards, since these immediately concerned the Communion Service; but there can be no doubt that, among a section of High Churchmen, a general revival of interest in the observance of religious customs in general is noticeable so far back as the earlier half of the century.

Miss Phebe Byrom died in 1785. In *Manchester Collectanea* (Chetham Soc.), vol. i, p. 213, Mr. Harland mentions as existing in Market Place in 1772 a 'man-mercer's' called 'Byrom's shop'; a note quotes the Directory of 1773 for 'Miss Phoebe Byrom, 1 Shambles;' and that of 1781 for the same, 'milliner, Market Place.']

DEAR Mrs. Phebe,　　if you will keep Lent,
　　We must, the Parsons say, be abstinent:
That is, we must abstain from certain things,
And live like Beggars rather than like Kings;
Tho', if we keep our Lent without a fuss,
No Monarch will live pleasanter than us.
Therefore, from Fish of every kind, and Eggs,

7. This is a fast after the fashion of the Greek Church where, in Lent, 'the faithful give up flesh meat, and confine themselves to the use of cheese and other *lacticinia*.' (Cf. Archbp. Dowden, *The Church Year and Calendar* (Cambridge, 1910, p. 84). On the Wednesday before Ascension Day (as a *dies profestus*) oil, wine and fish are allowed. *Ib.* i, p. 87. The Armenians, on fast days, abstain from flesh, milk, butter, eggs and oil. *Ib.*, p. 91.

And joynts of Meat, Breast, Shoulders, Necks and Legs—
And, what will more than all the rest avail,
We must avoid the Dish call'd Pot of Ale,   10
Sack, Tent, or Rhenish, in short, Wine or Brandy,
Whether from Bull's-Head, Coffee-house or friend Gandy.
Nor shall we want, with tolerable care,
Good meat and drink enough, and doughty fare.
For, while they sell Potatoes at our door,
We need not fear, or doubt of being poor;
And, while the Spring, the River, and the Pump
Afford us Drink, our Witts will always jump;
For diff'rence in Opinion does indeed
From diff[e]rence of Drink, as one may prove, proceed.   20
Do not the Torys, who drink Cookson's Ale,
Tell and believe years round the self-same Tale?
And Whiggs that guzzle down Frank Damport's gill,
Talk of King George, of Plots and Pop'ry still.
If Lady's deal in Scandal all the Day,
Blame not the Ladies; 'tis the effect of Tea;
The Men themselves, were they to drink of Green,
Wou'd in a minute be o'errun with Spleen;
Or, if Bohea they sip instead of Green,

8. The ellipsis almost seems to suggest—'Good Lord, deliver us!'

11. *Tent* (*vino tinto*), a dark-Spanish wine.

12. *Bull's Head*, a Manchester tavern frequented by Byrom and his set. Cf. *Remains*, vol. i, p. 319. (I cannot identify 'friend Gandy,' unless he be the John Gandy whom in 1730 the quaker E. Lampe mentions as a sympathiser in a letter to Byrom vol. ii. App., p. 592.)

14. *Doughty* : satisfactory (*tüchtig*).

21. *Cookson's Ale*, Cf. ante, *An Invitation to Breakfast*, l. 4.

23. *Frank Damport's gill*, cf. *Ib.*, l. 7. A 'gill' is half-a-pint, so in Lancashire at this day; or, according to Johnson, a quarter of a pint.

24. *Plots.* Such as 'Atterbury's Plot' (1722).

Colds and crude Vapours wou'd affect their Brain.   30
Coffee, you know's the Politician's liquor;
And who drinks Bottle Ale? The Country Vicar.
Thus different Tempers different liquors sip,
From Tent and Brandy down to Penny-whip.

31. Because of the expense of tea or coffee, of course.

32. From its association with coffee *houses*, which flourished most when party politics were at their height, in the Augustan age.

34. *Penny-whip,* small-beer sold at a penny a bottle.

A LETTER TO HIS WIFE AT KERSAL.

BEING WRIT OUT OF HAND, AND SENT BY MRS. PHEBE BYROM,
WHO WAS TAKING A WALK THITHER, AND DESIRED HIM TO
WRITE TO THEM; UPON WHICH HE WROTE THE FOLLOWING
LINES:

[This letter seems to belong to the period when, during
Byrom's frequent absences on 'shorthand' business in
London or Cambridge, his young wife and their children
occasionally stayed at Kersal with her father (cf. *Remains*,
vol. i, p. 357). This was after the earliest part of their
married life; for, in 1723 (two years after their marriage), he
writes to her, playfully bidding her 'set the bells a ringing,
hang the streets with tapestry, and so forth' on his return
home (*ib.*, p. 58), and in 1725 they abode together in
Manchester (*ib.*, pp. 175 *sqq.*). In 1727, he asks her "Don't
you choose to live at Kersall a little now and then?' (*ib.*,
p. 263). In 1728, he supposes 'you are all well at your
father's house and your own' (*ib.*, p. 289); and, later in the
year, he spent some time in his own house (*ib.*, p. 314).
Whether at this time Byrom already resided in Hanging
Ditch, where he afterwards had a house, must be left
uncertain; in his later years he lived in Fennel Street. Cf.
below, p. 57, *The Perils of Hunter's Croft*.]

THESE hasty Lines I send to wish thee, Wife,
    Health, and the pleasures of a Country Life;
Which, if thou taste, will soften to thy Spouse
The dull Confinement of an empty House—
Dull, empty House, where the mop'd Cat and I
Pass the long Hours most solitarily.

I hum the Twitcher o'er, and Puss cries 'Mew,'
To the same tune no doubt, viz., Absent You;
For ev'ry Place your Absence does confess:
Hall, Entry, Kitchen, Parlour great and less.   10
Deserted Kitchen! How thy once bright Grate
In dust and ashes mourns its present state;
While Tongs and Poker, Fire-shovel and Bellows
Look like four hanging, swinging rusty Fellows;
And all th' inferior Utensils about
In pensive silence speak the Fire gone out!
But most of all the Gentlemen of Metal,
Methinks, I pity the forlorn Tea-Kettle.
He never wanted, by thy Favour, Dame,
The constant Influence of the genial Flame;   20
Now, thrown aside, he lives neglected by,
The fate of Fav'rites to exemplify;
Never, no, never, must he hope to burn
'Till the glad Day that's fix'd for thy return.
Hard fate, indeed! For who cou'd e'er have thought
This restless vessel shou'd have had such Lot?
I never could believe, I must confess,
This moveable cou'd e'er be motionless.

7. *The Twitcher.* The celebrated character of Jimmy Twitcher in *The Beggars' Opera* (first acted in 1727) has no song in the play. As is well known, a passage in the play reflecting on Jimmy's good faith as a friend was exultantly applied by the public to the Earl of Sandwich's action against his former companion John Wilkes, and a large number of squibs against Sandwich as Jimmy Twitcher made their appearance; but this was at a much later date than the production of Byrom's lines.

14. Such a sight may not have been unfamiliar in Byrom's days; no further back than 1717 five Jacobite rebels taken at Preston were hanged there, traditionally at Knott Mill (Axon, *Annals of Manchester*, p. 76).

22. If these lines were written about 1728 or 9, there was no example very near at hand—at least in English political history—by which to illustrate them.

AN EPIGRAM BY MARTIAL IMITATED.

[The epigram imitated is n⁰· ccviii in bk. xiv : *Notarius.*
   Currant verba licet, manus est velocior illis;
     Nondum lingua suum, dextra peregit opus.
  (My words run fast, thy fingers run still faster;
   And hand of scribe outstrips the tongue of master.)

The term *notarius* is used by Quintilian and others of a
scribe who uses abbreviations, *i.e.*, a shorthand-writer.
There is no need for recalling here the important part played
by Shorthand in Byrom's earlier career; the first mention
of it in his *Remains* occurs in a letter written by him from
Cambridge in 1715; his proposals for publishing his system
were issued by him in 1723; in 1724 he became a Fellow of
the Royal Society, where he read papers on Shorthand, and
in 1742 a private bill was passed securing to him the sole right
of publishing his system (see *The Gentleman's Magazine* for
1742, p. 329). His *Universal Shorthand* was not, however,
actually published till 1767, four years after his death. The
happiest result of his labours in his art was that they brought
him into close contact with a large circle of friends in
Cambridge, London and Manchester, whom he enrolled as
members of the Shorthand Club, or 'Order,' and who
honoured him, nominally as their Grand Master, but of course
really because of his moral worth, his intellectual ability, and
his genius for friendship. Cf. the piece following the present,
entitled *Floreat Lex*, and notes.]

I.

'COME hither, Youth, whose nimble hand
   Can thus thy shorthand Strokes command;
Thou rare Assistant, whose device
Dispatches Business in a trice;
Come, take thy book and write my thoughts,
Thou that tak'st down with lines and dotts
Long phrases, without more ado,
As quickly as a word or two !

II.

'Tho', when I take my book and read,
My tongue exerts its utmost Speed,   10
And o're thy Ears, like patt'ring hail,
The quick successive sounds prevail—
Thy hand along the waxen Sea
Flies without either Stop or Stay,
And points my Words at ev'ry Stroke
With less Confusion than I spoke.

III.

'Or, tho' I speak what I conceive
Fast as my Tongue will give me leave,
Thou see'st at once unto what End
My round-about Expressions tend,   20
And find'st a cunning way to get
The words I scarce have spoken yet.
Wou'd I were able to indite
Or think, as fast as thou canst write!

IV.

'How is't that thus my thoughts betray
Or tell thee what I mean to say?
Strange, that within my very heart
Thy hand shou'd exercise its Art!
A new, inverted order this
Of things and their Proprietys,   30
That words should reach thy Ears so long
Before they pass the Speaker's Tongue!'

13. This old pronunciation is too well known to need remark. Cf. *To Mrs. Phebe Byrom*, l. 26, *ante*.

30. The use of ' propriety ' in the sense of ' property ' is frequent in our best sixteenth century writers. See in *Paradise Lost*, bk. iv, l. 751, the invocation to wedded love :—

'. . . sole propriety
In Paradise of all things
common else.'

V.

"No force of Learning, or of Use,
Can e're such strange Effects produce;
No hand can do it, in the Quill
As expeditious as it will.
'Tis Nature, or some Power Divine
That makes my thoughts run after Thine:
My Tongue does but obey thy Wit,
Obliged to speak what thou hast writ."   40

35. *In the Quill* : in mere penmanship.

FLOREAT LEX!

[This poem, which (see stanza VII) must have been written before December 7th, 1727, the date year of Ralph Leycester's marriage (see *Remains*, vol. i, p. 284), is conceived in a charming vein of mock gravity, with real urbanity beneath, befitting the whole organisation of the Shorthand Order, which called its meetings Chapters and its president Grand-Master. For the names of divers 'Brethren' of the Manchester Branch of the Club see the lines to the Rev. John Haddon and the Rev. Thomas Heywood, *ante*, vol. i, pp. 90-3, and cf. the preceding poem, and *Remains*, vol. i, pp. 315-7. The last couplet of the present stanzas admirably exemplifies Byrom's lighter poetic art and the irresistible 'dancing' of his diction, as it weaves itself into verse.]

I.

THE Accession of Egerton Leigh, Brother John,
    Is a Matter of Joy to us, every one;
As it does the Art credit to see it embrac't
By a man of his Character, Temper and Taste.

1. The Rev. Egerton Leigh, LL.D., eldest son of the Rev. Peter Leigh of West Hall in High Leigh, and of his wife Elizabeth, daughter of the Hon. Thomas Egerton, of Tatton Park, third son of John, second Earl of Bridgewater, was born 1702, LL.B., graduated from St. John's College, Cambridge, 1728; LL.D. 1743; *ob.* 1760, as Archdeacon of Salop. See notes to *Remains*, vol. i, p. 440, and vol. ii, p. 352.

1b. *Brother John* is the Rev. John Swinton, as to whom see *ante*, vol. i, p. 90 *note*.

When I saw the Dean Rural of Toft t' other day,
'We shall have a new Brother,' he seemèd to say.
Now I'm glad you confirm what he gave but a hint on,
By Advice from yourself, O my worthy Friend Swinton!

II.

So then, you have giv'n him, as I understand,
The Byromian Alphabet into his hand,   10
The contrivance of which—so exact and so nice,
So exceedingly plain, yet so vastly concise;
So simple, so lineal, so neat, and so forth—
Will apprize him, I hope, of its Use and its Worth,
And engage him to practise it, Even and Morn,
'Till the Pulpital Cushion it rise to adorn.

III.

Your hoping my Pardon for boldly proceeding
Without my Commission shows very good Breeding;
Your Distinction of Duty by 'formal' and 'real,'
That your Manner of thinking is just and ideal;   20
And this Mark of Esteem for myself and our Art
We take, as Grand Master, in very good Part.
For these, honest Culprit, and other like causes,
Your Pardon is fill'd up with Thanks and Applauses.

IV.

Then, as to the Title and Stile of Sub-Dean:
To be under Sir Peter's old rural demesne,
Your Ambition that prompts you to ask for a Post
Or your Love to the Squire shall I magnify most?

5. 'The Rural Dean of Toft' was a jocund designation of 'Sir Peter.'

16. *The Pulpital Cushion*, as it did, no doubt, in the case of many of the clerical members of the Shorthand Club.

25. *Sub-Dean*. This title is obviously also jocular.

26. *Demesne* is land which a man holds originally from himself, as 'Sir Peter' held the facetiously invented 'rural deanery.'

To unite in one Temper two Passions so distant,
That Philosophers hold to be hardly consistent,   30
And the Acid of Glory so nicely correct
By the Alkaline Nature of friendly Respect !

V.

This Title we therefore determine to give ye,
By and with the Advice of our Counsellors Privy;
And you, the said John, with full Pow'r to dispute,
To act in our Name at the Ford of Canute;
The Secreto-sagacious to hear and admit;
To do all things, in short, as your Wisdom thinks fit—
And this with the same Tachygraphical Vigour
As tho' our own Sprite did inhabit your Figure.   40

VI.

Mr. Dean will be glad of so good a Subaltern,
Whose Affairs, I presume, take a Connubiál turn.
To judge by the Object of Peter's Amours,
His thoughts are, no doubt, as ideal as yours;
His Norris, if Fame blows her Trumpet aright,
Will absorb Mr. Dean in a World of Delight.
May he long live possesst of the beautiful Samplar,
And his joys every Moment grow ampler and ampler !

VII.

Now, your Master and Scholar dispatch'd, I begin
With the points you desir'd to be satisfied in.   50
These, Mr. Sub-Dean, which in Number be two,
Are included in one Prepositional View.

31. *Correct*=corrected.
36. *The Ford of Canute*. Knutsford, whence Swinton writes to Byrom, *Remains*, vol. i, p. 284.
37. *The Secreto-sagacious*, the sagacious members of an occult fraternity.
45. *His Norris*. Ralph Leycester married Katharine, daughter and co-heiress of Edward Norris of Speke, Esq.
47. *Samplar*. A sampler is defined by Johnson as ' a piece worked by young girls for improvement'; here the word seems used in the sense of ' samplermaker '—unless indeed she had presented one to the Dean.

In the first, you adjust that particular Tribe,
Super, *Circum* and *Sub*, like an excellent Scribe;
For the very same Reason, it will be no wonder
If the second should save *Ante, Inter* and *Under*.

VIII.

And thus, to prevent all Misprision of Treason,
My Authority stamps what you argue from Reason—
Two things which in Short-hand we never divorce,
Since 'tis Reason that gives our Authority Force;　　60
And, if ever Dame Liberty spake from a Throne,
'Tis in mine I pretend that her Voice may be known :
What my Subjects acknowledge I only decide,
And from deeper Experience presume to be guide.

IX.

By our Letters and Rules, wheresoever, Dear Brother,
We can really distinguish one word from another,
There we lawfully take a true regular freedom
And use such contractions as oft as we need 'em.
Like Nature herself, we should write in our schools
By the shortest of Lines and the fewest of Rules—
And don't we already?　Come forth, thou Objection;
For we'll stop not an inch on this side of Perfection.　70

X.

Thus, Mr. Sub-Dean, I have answer'd your Letter.
For the rest, Brother Cattell is gotten much better.
His, and other Friends', Illness has hinder'd the Rhime
From waiting upon you two stages of Time.
But, for Rhiming itself, what Excuse?　Why, in short,
I must quote an anonymous Anecdote for't;
'When a Man's in a Humour too Merry for Prose,
His Words will be dancing in Spite of his Nose.'

72. *Brother Cattell*: the Rev.　*ante*, vol. i, p. 91 *note*.
Thomas Cattell, as to whom see

A TALE.

[It would be interesting to know, could it be ascertained,
when the custom of ending local proclamations of an unofficial
sort, including play-bills and the like, by the invocation
'God Save the King!' was first introduced, and whether it
was, in some cases, intentionally omitted in towns and other
places Jacobitically inclined.]

AN arch and sturdy Bell-man of the Town,
  That used to cry his Matters up and down,
As custom had not introduced the thing,
Never concluded with 'God Save the King!'
A blust'ring Captain, quarter'd in the Place
By where the Bell-man daily trod his Pace,
Took it as his Commission to correct
Of civil rule so crying a Neglect.
One day, as honest Stentor passing by
Had finished of his Catalogue the Cry,   10
'Hark ye,' says he; 'yon Bell-man, come up Stairs—
A Dog! I'll teach him how to cry his Wares!—'
Up goes the Man, into a public Room,
Where was the Captain, strutting in a fume.
The man thought, some Deserter or another
Had put the Hero into such a Pother.
"Sir," says he, bowing, as with Hat in hand,
"May't please your Worship, what is your command?"
'Command, ye Dog! If I were to preside,
I'd break the bones in your rebellious hide!'   20
"Bones, Sir? break bones?" (and then put on his Hat)
"What have I done, Sir? what d'ye mean by that?

7-8. Took it as part of his
military duty to correct such a
neglect of civil administration.
The pun on 'crying' (l. 12) is
good.

9. The Homeric herald Stentor
suggested to the author of *Hudibras* (part iii, canto i, l. 252).
  'The Stentrophonic voice
  That roar'd far off.'

I'm but a Bell-man; but, for all your Buff,
As good as you, Sir, and can look as Bluff.''
The Captain, not expecting such rebuke,
Began to soften his enragèd look;
Smooth'd on his brow the military frown,
And drop'd his Wrath to gentler Reason down:
'Pray, when you ring your bell about here, Friend,
And cry your Stuff—why don't you at the End   30
Pray for his Majesty, King George?' "I pray?"
Replies the Bell-man; 'O good lack a-day!
I pray, forsooth—and why not preach as well?
Is it to Pray'rs you think we ring our Bell?
Tho' I could pray as well as you can swear,
'Tis not my office.—Master, howsome'er,
I thought you wanted to have something cry'd!'
"Well, but, my friend" (the red-coat spark reply'd),
"In other Places, when the Bell is rung,
King George is pray'd for—here you hold your   40
  tongue.
Look ye, I've listen'd as I walk'd about,
And constantly have known you leave it out.
I eat his bread, and do insist that you
Pray for his Majesty, as others do;
Or else I'll"— 'Master, don't be in a Splutter;
You may eat bread and never fórsake butter—
What's that to me? And if you are, good Sir,
So fond of praying as you make a stir
(Which I much question), yet, if that's the Case,
The Church, Sir, not the Market, is the Place.   50
If this be all you have to say, farewell!'
And so, the Bell-man—bore away the Bell.
When he was gone, the Captain, quite abash'd
To find his Bill against the Bell-man quash'd,
To blunt in conversation, by degrees,

23. *Buff,* military attire. (A
buff-coat was a military coat
made of buffalo-leather.)

46. This recalls the converse
Scottish proverb: ' Mony care
for meal that hae baken bread
eneugh.'

The Edge of Stentor's cutting Repartees,
"Pray," says he, speaking to a stander by,
"Is it not usual at the Bell-man's cry
To pray 'God save the King?'" 'No, Sir; not here;
It is a custom which they have elsewhere;   60
But to these parts it is not yet come down;
At least, I never heard it in this Town.'
"You have in others?"—'Aye, Sir, several times.
It is a thing as common—as the Chimes.
Once, in particular, it made me smile.'
"How so?"—'I'll tell ye; but, in the meanwhile,
A Story, Sir, without offence begun,
If taken otherwise————I've done.'
"Well, Sir, go on!" 'Why, once, in such a place
There liv'd a Bell-man us'd to say this Grace,   70
Which ours know nothing of, it should appear—'
"An ignorant Rascal!" 'Nay, if you won't hear,
My tale is ended. I meant, not to revive,
But bury, that which does no good alive;
For Heat and Passion—' "Well, Sir, I have done."
'This Bell-man—Jack they called hm—(to go on)
Had orders once to cry a Carrier's horse,
Stray'd or convey'd out of its proper course;
So, to his work Jack went and rang his Bell:
"I want a horse"—and then began to tell
The Horse's Colour, Height, his Age and Straddle,
But quite forgot his wearing a Pack-saddle.   80
This special Token did not (thro' Confusion
Of Memory) occur till the Conclusion;
And Prayer was ended, so you're pleased to call it,
When, recollecting, thus we heard him bawl it
(Cart before horse a little), and the folks
About the market laughed), and crack'd their Jokes:
"God bless his Majesty, King George," says Jack;
Then roar'd forth--"with a Pack-saddle on his Back."

68. Perhaps a strong expres- is omitted here, at the expense
sion on the part of the Captain of the metre.

PET AND TEMPER.

[It is not easy to imagine such conduct as is here ascribed to the aggressor in a one-sided quarrel as having occurred, of all places in world, at a musical gathering in Manchester, where the first stone of the Gentlemen's Concert Room in Fountain Street was laid by Colonel Edward Greaves (as to whom see the lines *On the Marriage of Edward Greaves, Esq.*, below) in 1775, only twelve years after Byrom's death, and where, two years later was held the earliest known three days' 'musical festival' (cf. Axon, *Annals of Manchester*, pp. 103 and 104).]

TWO Sons of Music, at a Concert once,
   Diff'ring awhile, one call'd the other 'Dunce,'
'Blockhead,' and 'Fool,' as rising Passion taught.
The other kept his tongue, and answer'd naught;
And, to the question of the standers-by,
How he could take such words, and not Reply,
"Why, I would take," says he, "with all my heart
On any other Instrument a part;
But, if a man will play upon the Pet,
Solo, I think, is better than Duett."   10

9. The etymology of the substantive 'pet,' which is used, in the sense of a fit of peevishness, by Milton, while the adjective 'pettish' is to be found in Shakspeare, remains uncertain or unknown. But, surely, the meaning of the word is near enough to that of 'petulancy' to justify the conjecture that it was originally a colloquial abbreviation of this word, which was of Elizabethan usage.

DRYBONES, DAPPER AND LUCY.

[If, as one would gladly see reason for doubting, these lines are by Byrom, the apposite date 'April 1st 1783,' which does not appear in the Raines MSS. copy, must have been added by an earlier transcriber. Oysters and dances have always been popular in Manchester; but the combination of the two kinds of treat, though old-fashioned, is far removed from the traditional horse-play by which 'All Fools' Day' was long celebrated. The names of the interlocutors—including that of the 'sprightly' Lucy—cannot be traced to any individuals. 'Drybones' may be supposed to be a member of a profession for the practice of which Byrom, who had scant experience of it, also lacked inclination. Dapper, in Ben Jonson's *Alchemist*, is a lawyer's clerk of small understanding.]

Nunc pede libero
Pulsanda Tellus.
[Hor. *Od.*, bk. i, *Od.* xxxvii.]

S AYS Drybones to Dapper : ' 'T were a monstrous Bore
   To invite the young Girls to a Dance and to Oysters :
Th' idéa would shock, and at least half a score
   Would take prudish Refuge in Nunnery Cloysters.'

"That's right," replies Dapper; "in the Moon of All Fools
   We should not suggest one Idéa salacious;
A Shell-club each férmenting Crudity cools,
   For the Oyster-shells make a good Powder testaceous."

'Alas! Poor old England!' cries Lucy the sprightly,
   'What hopes of thy good when mere Shells are in   10
      fashion!
Time was when *thy* Friends were as vig'rous as sightly
   And could do more than dance in support of the Nation!

Let us shew our Contempt of such April-Fools,
   Nor stoop to such Nothings, our favours to sell!
Who would idly caress such inanimate tools
   And, in lieu of the Oysters, take up with the Shell?'

---

8. *Powder testaceous*. Probably used as a medicament, like ground ivory.

9. It is not easy to apprehend the sprightly young lady's point. Could she have had in her mind a ghastly meaning of the word ' shells ' ?

ON WILLIAM III'S HORSE SORREL.

[The Latin lines translated by Byrom were sent by Dr. Thomas Smith, a learned divine, among whose many publications are noted a *Catalogue of the Cottonian MSS.* and a *Life of Sir Robert Cotton*, to Samuel Pepys, with a letter dated April 16th, 1702 (*Diary and Correspondence of Samuel Pepys*, ed. Mynors Bright, vol. vi (1879), p. 241. Inasmuch as Dr. Smith describes the lines as 'some few heroic lines upon *Sorrell*; which, after a single reading, I presume you will throw in the fire,' 'J.Y.', in *Notes and Queries*, 2d ser., vol. i, p. 487, is probably right in conjecturing that they, and presumably also the 'Epitaph upon the late high and mighty Dutch Hero' which accompained them,' were Dr. Smith's own composition. Macaulay's account of the incident celebrated in this cold-blooded effusion is as follows :
'On the twentieth of February (1702 N.S.) William (III) was ambling on a favourite horse, named Sorrel, through the park of Hampton Court. He urged his horse into a gallop just at the spot where a mole had been at work. Sorrel stumbled on the mole-hill, and went down on his knees. The King fell off, and broke his collar-bone. The bone was set ; and he returned to Kensington in his coach. The jolting of the rough roads of that time made it necessary to reduce the fracture again. To a young and vigorous man such an accident would have been a trifle. But the frame of William was not in a condition to bear even the slightest shock.' (*History of England*, chap. xxv.) William died early on March 8th.
Curiously enough, the horse Sorrel had formerly belonged to Sir John Fenwick, as to whom see l. 6 of Byrom's translation below. The Jacobites used to drink healths to 'Sorrel,' and to toast 'the little gentleman in a suit of black velvet,' meaning the mole that threw up the heap which caused the

horse to stumble and fall.   See 'W.D.' in *Notes and Queries*, 2d ser., vol. ix, pp. 486–7, who also informs us that 'a sorrel horse is a kind of roan, that would now be called a strawberry.'   In the Jacobite *Willie Winkie's Testament*, Willie Winkie (a Jacobite nickname for King William III) makes various bequests (after the manner of Villon or Dunbar) to 'Fader Denison,' and says

> 'Tak you moreover, Denison,
> De cursed horse dat broke dis bone.'

(See *Jacobite Songs and Ballads*, ed. G. S. Macquoid, 1888). 'J.Y.', *u.s.*, also states that, according to Miss Strickland, *The Queens of England*, vol. viii, p. 120, edn. 1854, Pope's lines

> Angels that watched the Royal Oak so well
> How chanced ye nod, when luckless Sorel 'fell,'

remained in MS. till after the poet's death.   See note on *Epilogue to the Satires. Dial.* ii, l. 227, 17, Pope's Works, Elwin and Courthope's edn., vol. iii, p. 486.   Cf. *ib.*, vol. vii, p. 81, Gay's heartless paraphrase of the herb sorrel as 'that which killed King Will.']

In equum, ex quo dejectus Auriacus peviit.

ILLUSTRIS Sonipes! certe dignissime Coelo;
Cui Leo, cui Taurus, cui daret Ursa locum!
Quae te felicem felicia Prata tulerunt?
Ubera quae felix praebuit alma parens?
Hibernis patrium venisti ulturus ab oris;
Aut Glenco, aut stirps te Fenniciana dedit.
Sis felix quicunque, precor, memorande, nec unquam
Jam Sella dorsum Frena nec ora premant.
Humani generis Vindex, moriente Tyranno,
Hanc Libertatem, quam dabis, ipse tene!   10

8. *Sella tuum, conj.*   10. *Dabas, conj.*

The above translated into English by the late Dr. Byrom:

I LLUSTRIOUS Horse! for thee the starry sphere
    Might change the Bull, the Lion, and the Bear.
Thy lucky Birth what happy Pastures claim?
What glorious Dam hath nurs'd thee up to Fame?
• Its wrongs Hibernia bred thee to requite,
    Or Glenco's breed, or Fenwick's, gave thee Light.
Blest be thy Lot! Henceforth, enjoy the Plain;
No Saddle press thy Back, no Bit restrain!
Mankind aveng'd, the Tyrant overthrown,
Thou gav'st us Freedom, let it be thy own!   10

5. The reduction of Ireland to submission, 1689—91, was in part effected by William III. in person.

6. William III. certainly desired an example to be made of the Macdonalds of Glencoe, if they could be proved to be excluded from the indemnity; though the method of the 'Massacre' itself was, as a matter of course, not under his control. Sir John Fenwick was executed in January, 1697, for his share in, or cognisance of, the Assassination Plot of 1695.

A MANCHESTER MEMORANDUM.

COPY OF A CARD SENT IN THE YEAR 17—- TO FRANCIS FUTURE,
ESQ.: MRS. MANCHESTER SENDS HER COMPLIMENTS, AND
DESIRES HIS ACCEPTANCE OF A MEMORANDUM.

[These lines undoubtedly refer to the Manchester Workhouse Bill, which was thrown out in 1731, largely through
Byrom's exertions. Cf. the lines *On the Whig Workhouse
Bill, ante*, vol. i, pp. 220-1, with introductory note, and the
references to *Remains*. For a correction of this note see
below, *Addenda et Corrigenda to vols. i and ii*. Cf. also
Aikin's *Description of the Country . . . round Manchester*
(1795), p. 215; where the opposition to the Bill in London is
said to have been conducted by Byrom in conjunction with
Thomas Pigott, Esq., barrister-at-law, and where a letter by
Byrom is cited, half-prophetically varying the metaphor in
the superscription of these lines, and stating that he and his
associate 'looked upon themselves embarked in *the good ship
Manchester* and . . . ready to work as hard as if they were
never so considerable sharers in the cargo.'

Though buildings for a workhouse were erected in 1763,
when it was proposed to constitute Manchester a borough
(see the curious account in *Manchester Collectanea* (Chetham
Soc.), vol. ii, pp. 224-5), the scheme was defeated like that
of 1731; and a second generation passed before the first
Manchester workhouse was actually opened in 1793 (see
Axon's *Annals of Manchester*, pp. 95 and 118)].

LET Bills contriv'd for Public good
   Be soon and fairly understood !
Tho' Privacy be somewhat snugger
That brings them in by Hugger Mugger :
Yet, as it makes the People surly,
We'll throw 'em out—by Hurly Burly.

THE PREFERMENT.

An Epigram.

[This ill-natured epigram, in which conventional spite does duty for wit, must have been written when Sir Robert Walpole, who had been made Knight of the Bath on May the 27th, 1725, became Knight of the Garter on May 26th, 1726. The Order of the Bath had been revived in the former year, no doubt with a view to facilitate the carrying on of the government; the Garter had not for more than two generations been bestowed upon a commoner, and 'Sir Bluestring' was held up to scorn in consequence. (See *Dictionary of National Biography*, vol. lix, p. 190.) Had the honour not been granted when it was, Walpole might have had to wait for it some little time, for in 1727 George II succeeded his father.]

SIR Robert, his Merit and Int'rest to show,
    Laid down his Red Ribbon to put on the Blue;
In two Strings, already, the Knight is preferr'd:
Odd numbers are lucky—we wish him a third!

ON THE THANKSGIVING DAY.

[Among the Jacobite papers preserved in the Raines MSS. xxxiv, p. 80, is the following letter addressed by 'Sam Norris' to Thomas Ferrand, Attorney-at-Law in Rochdale. 'Sam Norris' was probably connected with the Rev. John Norris, Fellow of All Souls' College, Oxford, and Rector of Bemerton, an eminent divine who as a moral philosopher belongs to the school of the 'Cambridge' Platonists. (For notices of him see *Remains*, vol. i, p. 632, *note*, and *Dictionary of National Biography*, vol. xli, pp. 132–4.) Byrom (*Remains, u.s.*) speaks of a conversation concerning Norris at Cambridge, at which 'Ferrand' was present. This was no doubt the Rev. Thomas Ferrand, of Trinity College, Cambridge, mentioned by Byrom in 1723 as 'Parson Ferrand' (see *Remains*, vol. i, p. 51, and note), with whom Thomas Ferrand of Rochdale may, in his turn, be presumed to have been connected.

Together with this letter, there is pasted, on p. 80 of the MS. volume where it is inserted, another letter, from Thomas Ferrand, giving an account of the passage of the Scottish troops through Rochdale, on their way to Manchester, dated (perhaps in a moment of agitation) 'November 31st, 1745.'

Mr. Norris writes as follows :

'Good Sir,
The two following Epigrams I receiv'd last [here some words are torn off in the MS.] Friend of mind [*sic*], which I think will not be disagreeable to you and some other Rochdale Worthies.'

Then follow the two epigrams, of which the first is that here printed, while the other is, with no variations of importance, Byrom's famous 'God bless the King' etc. (for which see vol. i, pp. 572, *ante*), here entitled 'On toasting the King.' In *Appendix B* of his *Biography of Thomas Deacon* (Manchester, 1911), Mr. H. Broxap cites the following extract from the *Chester Courant*, 28th October, 1746 :

"Manchester, October 21st. The 9th inst. being the day appointed for a Public Thanksgiving was observed here with all the marks of loyalty and joy suitable to so glorious and happy an occasion. There is among us a poor woman, Mrs Siddall, late wife to one of the unhappy persons whose heads have been fixed up here* and at present a distressed widow, deprived of her family's chief support and burthened with five young children, who being too much swallowed up in her own private calamity to enter into the public rejoicing or show any marks of joy upon an event, which though happy to the whole, is melancholy and fatal enough, God knows, to her, neglected to light her candles : upon which a party of soldiers along with some townsmen assaulted her house in the most violent and outrageous manner, not only breaking the windows and demolishing the shutters and the very frames of the sashes, but even threatening to lay it level with the ground : so that she was forced to fly with her children to a neighbour's house and to leave her own to their mercy. The scandal too of this illegal injurious, and inhuman action was aggravated by its being done within six yards of the principal guard, the sentinel walking at the very door without

---

* Thomas Siddall or Sydall, executed on Kennington Common, July 30, 1745, as one of the officers in the Manchester regiment of rebels.

any offer to prevent it, and not forty from the house where the officers and civil magistrates were celebrating the day. I shall conclude with a piece of wit handed about here, severe indeed, but just enough, I must own, upon this occasion.

It is scarcely necessary to remark that the above composition, prose and verse alike, is universally attributed to John Byrom.

"Yours, PHILELEUTHERUS MANCUNIENSIS."]

BY the bare title of this Text, a Laick
    Would think the times were very Pharisaick :
Long Prayers to Heaven are in the morning pour'd ;
At Night, behold the Widow's house devour'd.

WARRINER'S FOLLY.

[The meaning of this title has proved undiscoverable, and the point of the epigram therefore remains obscure.   The barber's proposal to Queen Caroline could not but have been offensive to Her Majesty ; for 'the great Sir Watkin' was one of the most persistent foes of the Hanoverian dynasty, and pursued Queen Caroline's chosen minister Sir Robert Walpole with unrelenting animosity, attempting to renew an enquiry into his conduct of affairs so late as December 1743, after the efforts to impeach him had failed.   Concerning Sir Watkin Williams Wynn (1692—1749) who, as the great Tory chief of North Wales, sat in parliament for the last twenty-nine years of his life, and whom, when his complicity in the '45 was revealed, the Government did not venture to touch, see D. Lleufer Thomas' notice in vol. lxiii of *The Dictionary of National Biography*, and cf. the verses in his memory in vol. xix of *The Gentleman's Magazine* (for 1749), p. 470.

TO Her Majesty's presence a Barber advanc'd ;
    Says he : 'Let the Jig of Sir Watkin be danc'd !
But, as in our bosoms it raises a flame,
Pray, let it be call'd for by some other name !'
"No ; by its true name we will call it," says Dolly :
"You may, if you please, call it ' Warriner's Folly.' "

---

5. *Dolly.* No doubt Byrom's   rather than her aunt and name-
daughter Dorothy (b. 1730),   sake.

Perhaps, this may be as suitable a place as any other in which to cite the following note from the Raines MS. xlv, p. 43, where it is entered in Canon Raines' handwriting just before the lines superscribed '*Warriner's Folly*,' with which it has, of course, no imaginable connexion.

> Dr. Byfield, a chemist of an extravagant genius and the inventor of *Sal Volatile Oleosum* with whom the Author had frequent skirmishes of Wit and Humour at Richards' Coffee House, and, upon his Death, wrote the following short Epitaph, *impromptu* :—
> ' *Hic jacet Dr. Byfield, diu Volatilis, tandem fixus.*'

As to Byrom's 'skirmishes' with Byfield, see *Remains*, vol. i, pp. 51 and 52.

Dr. Norman Moore (to whom no appeal for information is ever made in vain) kindly tells me that the person whose epitaph Byrom wrote was T. Byfield, M.D., Fellow of the Royal College of Physicians in Dublin. He published in London in 1675 *A Short Discourse on the Rise, Nature and Management of the Small-Pox, etc., Occasioned by the Death of Our Late Incomparable Queen. Together with a Philosophical Remedy for these and many other diseases.* My informant, who describes this essay as apparently the work of a shallow enthusiast, adds that Byfield must be supposed to have come to London and to have practised there without any right to do so, thus coming to be known as a self-asserting, bumptious person. Hence the pamphlets *The Two Sosias, or the True Dr. Byfield at the Rainbow Coffee House, to the Pretender in Jermyn Street*, and a (supposed) *Letter to the Learned Dr. Woodward by Dr. Byfield* (dated from the Rainbow Coffee House in December 1718)—both published in London in 1719. These Byfield pamphlets, Dr. Norman Moore observes, are part of the Woodward cycle, to which belongs the *Letter from the facetious Dr. Andrew Tripe at Bath to his loving brother the Profound Greshamite*, attributed to Dr. William Wagstaffe (physician to St. Bartholomew's); and he thinks that they have nothing to do with T. Byfield, except that they make use of his name.]

O . . N v. THE KING OF FRANCE.

[On the whole, there seems no reason for excluding the following verses from the Byromic canon; though they contain an occasional inelegancy (ll. 4, 5, 8, 13, 16) or platitude, they are not without one or two happy turns, and the sentiment is such as he would not have disavowed. The piece evidently refers to attacks upon the Young Pretender and Louis XIV by a writer who was a Whig and Non-Conformist. I have no doubt that the letters O—n in l. 20 signify Owen—Josiah Owen of Rochdale, as to whom see interesting note to *Sir Lowbred O . . n*, vol. i, pp. 358 to 363, a vigorous non-conformist preacher and writer, who was a strong Anti-Jacobite and enemy of Rome, and with whom Byrom's friend Dr. Deacon, and through him Byrom himself, were in feud. The term 'farcio-sermonic' seems to have been applicable to some at least of his productions (see Mr. C. W. Sutton's *The Writings of 'Doctor' Thomas Deacon and his Opponent, the Rev. J. Owen*, Manchester, 1879.) His 'scandalous' sermon (as it is called by Halley) *All is well, or the Defeat of the late Rebellion*, preached at Rochdale on October 9th (1749), and printed in London, n.d., is preserved in Byrom's library. (In the *Catalogue* his name is given as *James* Owen.)]

WHAT Force of Oratory, Sir, is here;
    What genuine Reas'ning and what borrowed Sneer!
Historian, Preacher, Poet—all concur
To form the farcio-sermonic slur;
Against the poor Pretender to outstrike,
Fact, Eloquence and Humour—all alike!
But, to proceed, and see how he o'erthrows,

---

4. *Slur.* Presumably in the in that of 'trick'; but in neither sense of 'reproach' rather than a very suitable word.
    5. *Outstrike*, put forth.

Next place, the second of his ghostly foes!
One King, according to the learnèd Clerk ,
Pays the whole Mob—to wit, the *Grand Monarque.*   10
Born over Gallia's Empire to preside,
The well-belovèd or the well-belied—
Be which he will—his Reign is spent entire,
Like that of Lewis, his tyrannic Sire,
Wellnigh a cent'ry *both*, in forging chains
To bring all Europe under his Domains.
Europe, perhaps, divides the forgèd store,
And laughs at chains [such as] she never wore;
But we see plainly, in a case so trite,
Europe deceived, and O--n in the right.   20
Let Kings await the Judgment of his Bench :
He knows their Monarch better than the French.
Titles conferr'd by only Papal Bulls
He in full conventicle disannuls;
Unchristianises the Most Christian King,
And makes the Soundboard with 'French Tyrant' ring.
What Briton knows not that the French are slaves,
And their great Chief, however he behaves,
Tyrant, of course—and must be, by the bye,
Till some good Fortune makes him Our ally,   30
And, grown victorious in the common cause,
The *quondam* Tyrant merits our applause.

8. In the next place.

10. The *Grand Monarque.* The title of *Le Grand* was specially voted to Louis XIV. by the city of Paris in 1680.

12. Louis XV. was styled *Le Bien-Aimé* by his courtiers on the occasion of his recovery from the malady which befell him at Metz in 1744.

15. *Wellnigh a cent'ry both;* reckoning Louis XIV. from 1661 to 1715, and Louis XV. from 1724 to the date of these verses.

20. See *introductory note.*

24. The word is so accentuated both in Shakespeare and in later verse, *e.g.* :

' He us'd to lay about and stickle,
Like ram or bull, at Conventicle.'

Hudibras, pt. i, canto ii, l. 438.

Till then, with equal Justice we may brand
The 'Well-belovèd' Lewis and the 'Grand':
May upon Gallic Majesty, each mail,
Reflections base and scandalous retail;
Insults on Royalty till then may pass
Amongst the People of the lowest class:
Example, stronger than Advice, permits
The meanest and the most abandon'd wits   40
To vent low Ribaldry against the Throne
Of any Prince in Europe but their own.
As if that Prince's subjects could not fling
The like invective on a hostile King,
And soon afford Proofs, equally sublime,
Of British Freedom, in a Foreign Clime!
   Amongst the Demagogues of ev'ry Soil
There are who think it Genius to revile;
Who throw hard words together on a heap,
And purchase vulgar Reputations cheap.   50
To them a Mitre rail'd at, or a Crown,
Secures a load of infamous Renown,
That rises just as what they have defam'd
More Sacred Rev'rence, or more Civil, claim'd.

43. As if a retort against the King of Great Britain were not open to the subjects of any other sovereign attacked by a British writer! (The suggestion is a little too obvious not to betray intention.)

53. *Just as.* In exact proportion as.

D

AN EXTEMPORE PETITION GIVEN TO A POOR TURK WHO SOLICITED THE AUTHOR'S ASSISTANCE TOWARDS RANSOMING HIS WIFE AND CHILDREN.

[Byrom's compassionate nature seems to have induced him to write these lines for the use of an unlucky Turk, who had appealed to his kindness. We cannot fail to notice that it was Christian slavery to which the petitioner had been subjected at Malta. See a rather odd passage in Taaffe's *History of the Order of St. John of Jerusalem*, vol. iv, p. 175: ' In 1742 Vilhena died, and was succeeded [as Grand-Master] by Sir Pinto da Fonseca, who came to a long truce with the Sultan; excepting that each side retained their prisoners, who were in a sort of slavery. For against the spirit of the knights howsoever, yet, as the Turks would not relinquish that barbarous custom, it was forced upon the others as equitable reprisals,—which, if not a good reason, at least palliates a bad; besides to have galleys, how to do without galley slaves. . . . But many of these called slaves were raised from the galleys to far easier conditions,' etc.]

CHRISTIANS, behold a Stranger in Distress,
His hapless Case unable to express;
Merchant in Turkey, Slave in Malta made,
Ruin'd by what enriches others—Trade!
Four years a Slave, when, freed, he left behind
A Wife, two Sons, a Daughter, still confin'd;
Their Ranson now th' unhappy Father's aim,
To London in the first fraught Ship he came;
Now seeks Newcastle, where, to Traders known,

8. *Fraught ship,* ship that carried a freight.

He hopes to quit this Country for his own— 10
His own, where (tho' of Fortune now the scorn)
His friends confess him not ignobly born.
Weeping, perhaps, at present for the Fate
Of Him who stands thus helpless at your Gate,
How will they joy, when He shall cross the flood
And free from Bonds the Partners of his Blood,
Sunk by the griefs that all have undergone!
Let, let your kind assistance speed him on;
Speed him to join a Family restor'd,
And help the wand'ring Ransomer aboard! 20
Tho' dumb to such a distant Country's Speech,
His Look, his Air, his Habit all beseech;
By the Man's native, unaffected Mien
That which his Words refuse to tell is seen.
Cast on him, then, a favourable Eye;
Let Sense of Pity want of Sound supply;
Let the poor Merchant in Misfortunes know
That real Want, that Providential Woe,
Beyond all force of Language or of Art,
Can speak Compassion to an English Heart! 30

PHYSICIANS' MANNERS.

[The MS. adds at the conclusion of the following lines:
'From Pen's Practice of Physic, a MS. in the Radcliffe L.'
But, on enquiry at the Library, I find that no such MS. is
known there; and some jest may, therefore, be involved in
the note.

The lines have little point or significance, unless the
concluding '*probatum est*' be supposed to suggest some
personal reminiscence. Byrom, we may well believe, had
scant sympathy with bombastic arrogance like that of the

quack Dr. Misaubin, to whom Fielding dedicated his *Mock Doctor*, or pompous self-assertion like that of the two physicians who consult over the body of Captain Blifil in *Tom Jones*. For the rest, it is difficult to escape the impression that he had no real liking for the profession itself, which his Montpelier degree would have entitled him to practise. In 1727 he writes to his wife: 'I had yours dated 26th of June about practising physics at Manchester. . . . I have neither health enough, nor interest, nor experience, nor consequently inclination enough to practise physic at Manchester. . . . . . What, I pray, have the physicians at Manchester ever got, in proportion to that night and day slavery, 'pothecary slavery, registration slavery, disabling slavery, party slavery, etc., to which they are continually exposed?' (*Remains*, vol. i, p. 267)].

I.

A MAN disorder'd in his outward frame
Thou callest *Patient* by a proper name;
For, in his weak condition, Kill or Cure,
Thy management thereof he must endure.

II.

But, if thou lookest to receive a fee,
Thou must be patient, too, as well as he;
Must gently treat the Party that is ill,
And greet the House that honoureth thy skill.

III.

It may be great; they deem it so, no doubt,
Who send for thee to bring his cure about;   10
But, if thou fumest, and thy Brain be hot,
Behold, thy knowledge profiteth him not.

IV.

Blessing thereon thou canst not well expect,
For thy Behaviour curseth in effect;
And, if the man recovereth, in fine,
It must be owing to a Help—not thine.

V.

Careless of him, intent upon his Pelf,
If thou shalt stalk, and glorify Thy self,
Hector, and bounce, and (peradventure) swear,
Nor sick nor well can thy disorder bear.   20

VI.

The things of Nature will be out of course:
The Patient bad, and the Physitian worse;
Who heedeth not the salutary Plan
Of William Wykeham: 'Manners makyth Man.'

VII.

Doubly distrest, what shall the Household do,
Griev'd at the Sick—and at the Doctor, too?
Body and mind responsively unsound,
What Med'cine can there for the twain be found?

VIII.

Why, verily, if thou wilt yield thy Faith
To what the World, on such occasion saith: 30
'Another Doctor for the Man!—the Beast!
Get shut of him at once!'—*Probatum est.*

24. Byrom was interested in William of Wykeham, though, so far as I know, for no special reason. Cf. *Epitaph on William of Wykeham,* vol. i, pp. 554—893.

BROGUING.

[Here is another plea for good manners—this time against
intemperance in speech. The 'dear Thomas' to whom the
remonstrance is addressed it would be cruel (even were it
possible) to identify. The use, in this piece (vv. 25 and 32)
of the word 'brogue' to signify rough vituperation, without
any notion of dialogue being implied, is, to say the least,
uncommon. The examples given in *The Oxford English
Dictionary* seem more or less to apply to Irish speech. The
derivation of the word from 'brogues' (a Celtic kind of foot-
gear) is, however, unconvincing.]

I.

'DEAR Thomas, if I could but tell
    What kind of remedy would quell
This overflowingness of Gall,
Which thou art wont to pour on all,
Who do but once incur thy Hate,
I'd purchase it at any Rate;

II.

'To save the pain that friends and foes
Endure whene'er it overflows.
For Friends are sorrowful, to see
Such a relentless Wrath in thee;   10
And Foes grow desperate, to find
No mercy, though they change their mind.

III.

'Dame Nature has not made thee like
A slut, ill-natured, surly Tike;
But cheery, brisk and debonnair—

14. 'Base tike, callst thou me host?' *Ancient Pistol.*

Is it not, then, a strange affair,
Which no advantage rises from,
To make thyself so, honest Tom?

IV.

'Prithee, reflect a little Bit;
For it is neither fair nor fit,   20
Granting that others might be wrong,
To keep so vain a wrath so long!
What was, at first, but Heat and Passion
Grows downright Malice, on thy Fashion—

V.

'Bad, when at first provok'd, the Brogue:
"Dog! Villain! Scoundrel! Rascal! Rogue!"
But, ever after, worse and worse;
And, then, the Oath; and, then, the Curse;
And, then—too late, by the effect,
To mention—Prithee, Tom, reflect!'   30

VI.

"I will; I will; so, pray, give o'er;
The Broguing shall be mine no more!
Should I be tempted to offend,
I'll call to mind our Coleshill Friend,
And recollect, to stop the wrong,
The honest Mole-catcher's 'How LONG?'"

34 and 36. These allusions   least three Coleshills, all places
must remain dark. There are at   of some interest.

ON THE MARRIAGE OF EDWARD GREAVES, Esq.

[See *Remains*, vol. ii, p. 503: Robert Thyer to Byrom, Manchester, 31st July, 1749: 'You know, I suppose, that Mr. Egerton of Tatton is going to be married to Miss Copley, and his friend Mr. Greaves to Miss Lever.' Edward Greaves (afterwards Colonel Greaves), of Culcheth Hall (as to whose interest in music see introductory note to *Pet and Temper*, *ante*, p. 21), was the son of Edward Greaves (for a notice of whom by Canon Raines see Wilson's *Miscellanies*, in *Chetham Society's Publications*, vol. xlv, p. 68), and no doubt a connexion of William Greaves, of Fulbourne in Cambridgeshire, 'fast friend' of Bentley (see note to *Remains*, vol. i, p. 339), who died in 1783, aged 75, as one of the Feoffees of Chetham's Hospital. 'Matty' (Martha) Lever's parents were Sir Darcy and Lady Lever, of both of whom, as well as of their daughter, there were fine portraits, by Winstanley, at Alkrington. (See *note* to *Remains*, vol. ii, p. 407). Culcheth Hall had come into the possession of the Greaves family by the marriage of Edward's father, John Greaves, to Jane Gilliam. The piece is a happy instance of Byrom's lighter manner and its humorous insistance on the return of the wedded couple almost reads like a parody of '*Ducite ab urbe domum, mea carmina, ducite Daphnim.*']

Y OU think, perhaps, that you have cheated us,
    And quite escap'd all Matrimonial fuss?
No; you mistake: whene'er you come again,
Tho' wrong'd at present, we'll revenge it then;
We shall regard you as new-married folk,
On whom Friend Crouchley has just tied the yoke.

6. The Rev. John Crouchley, elected Fellow of the Manchester Collegiate Church in 1757, died in 1760. (See *Remains*, vol. ii, p. 60, and Raines' *Fellows of the Collegiate Church of Manchester*, vol. ii, p. 247.)

Put on your Ranelagh and Vauxhall airs,
Talk of your Op'ras and such like affairs—
We shall retain in Mem'ry, by your leaves,
Miss Matty Lever and Squire Edward Greaves :   10
An happy Match, if London does not spoil
The genuine product of our Native Soil.
   Return, return, ye wand'ring pair, return !
Think, for your sakes how friendly bosoms burn ;
How mine, for one, you well may think, must ake
To wear my Gloves, and eat my Bridal Cake,
And make an awkward show from hand to mouth,
While Bride and Groom are gone into the South !
   Return, I say, ye wand'ring Couple, home !
Settle, and House, and cease, henceforth, to roam !   20
If ye would keep your Promises for Life,
Of Loving Husband and obedient Wife :
Here, amongst us, let all your moments flow,
With all the bliss that Marriage can bestow !

16. *To   wear   my   gloves.*
' Gloves,' says J. W. Norton-
Kyshe, in his *Law and Customs
relating to Gloves* (1901), p. 86,
'are still occasionally given at
weddings. . . White wedding
gloves are mentioned by Dekker
in 1599, and after a wedding in
1604 the gloves given to the
guests cost nearly £1000.'

TO MR. LEVER.

[Mr., afterwards Sir Ashton, Lever, to whom this letter is addressed, was the eldest son of Byrom's early friend Sir Darcy Lever, of Alkrington near Middleton, as to whom see *Remains*, vol. i, p. 45 *note*.   He succeeded his father in 1742, when he must have been quite a young man (he is 'Master Ashton Lever' in 1736; cf. *ib*., vol. ii, p. 60).   If the present lines were written some time after his accession to title and estate, this would help to account for his eagerness to act as steward of the races.   A biography of him, published, with a portrait, in *The European Magazine and London Review* for August 1784 (vol. vi, pp. 83-5)—apparently with the idea of promoting the lottery, of which immediately—dwells on his 'early passion for excelling'; and he is said always to have a great love for horses, and to have been able to teach his hunters the tricks of the circus.   Indeed, his love of animals, and of natural objects in general, was the master passion of his life.   Besides keeping an admirably trained pack of beagles 'and pointers in great perfection,' he rendered his family-seat 'famous for the best aviary in the Kingdom, containing near 4000 birds, and became possessor of a very remarkable natural history museum.   (See letter in *The Gentleman's Magazine* dated November 25th, 1772, vol. xliii, p. 219.)   Dr. Axon informs me that a description in verse of the museum while still at Alkrington was written by James Ogden and printed in 1774, and that a copy of this is in the Manchester Reference Library.   Gradually, this museum attracted so many visitors, that the owner felt constrained to 'exclude those who came on foot; and, in 1775, he removed it to London, where he placed it in Leicester House, Leicester Square, and opened it to the public.   For lack, however, 'of suitable patronage' he found himself, in 1785, obliged to dispose of it by lottery, at a guinea a ticket. The prize was won by a Mr. Parkinson, who for a time exhibited the collection on the Surrey side of Blackfriars Bridge; but its items were ultimately sold by auction. (See Mr. C. W. Sutton's notice of Sir Ashton Lever in *Dictionary of National Biography*, vol. xxxiii (1893), and cf. Chalmers' *Biographical Dictionary* (1815), vol. xx, p. 219, and *The Gentleman's Magazine*, vol. lviii, part i, 1788.) In 1771, Sir Ashton Lever was High Sheriff. He died at Manchester, in 1788, from an apoplectic fit, when on the bench with other magistrates. (According to Axon, *Annals of Manchester*, p. 115, 'it has been surmised that his death was due to poison self-administered.')

The establishment of races on Kersal Moor in 1729 caused some controversy (*ib.*, p. 80). When, shortly afterwards, it was proposed to start a public subscription for the purpose of ensuring the continuance of the races, a strong protest was raised, which found expression, both vehement and pointed, in a pamphlet entitled *A Serious Dissuasive from an intended Subscription for continuing the Races upon Kersal Moore, address'd to the Inhabitants of Manchester and Parts adjacent*, of which a copy, in the third edition, 1733, is preserved in the Manchester Free Library. This pamphlet has been generally attributed to John Byrom. But Mr. H. Broxap (*Biography of Thomas Deacon, Appendix A*) attributes the authorship of *A Serious Dissuasive* not to John, but to his elder brother Edward Byrom, under whose name it is entered in John Byrom's intimate friend John Clayton's Manuscript Catalogue, though in the Free Reference Library Catalogue it appears as by John Byrom himself. The present poem, deals with the subject in the same vein as the pamphlet though with more moderation of tone. More especially, the appeal in the pamphlet to the gentry, as such, finds its echo in Byrom's verse. On the other hand, this contains no allusion either to the death of two men in a brawl on the race-course, to which the pamphlet refers, or to Bishop Peploe's prohibition of the appearance of any of his clergy at the Assemblies, which it mentions with approval. Byrom's pamphlet (assuming it to have been his) was answered in 1733 by *Remarks upon the Serious Dissuasive from an*

*Intended Subscription for continuing the Races etc. with
A Serious dissuasive Word to the Dissuader*, which is
attributed to the Rev. Thomas Cattell, Chaplain of the
Collegiate Church—the same who replied to Byrom's *Advice
to the Rev. Messrs. H— and H to Preach Slow* (vol. i,
pp. 101–5), by an admonition to them to preach fast. (See
Preface to the present volume; and cf., for an account of
Thomas Cattell, and of his friendly controversies with Byrom,
the passage there cited from Canon Raïnes' *Lives of the
Fellows and Chaplains of the College of Manchester*, part ii.
The pair were clearly firm friends, in spite of differences of
opinion, and were attracted towards one another by their common interest in stenography—and by their common Jacobit-
ism.) The reply is not unskilful, but illustrates the bitterness
with which zeal could be opposed by hatred of zeal. Mr.
Broxap (*u.s.*) adds that the *Remarks* attributed to Thomas
Cattell were followed by a comment of which Thomas Deacon
was the author, and which is entered under his name in John
Clayton's Catalogue as *Remarks upon the Remarker*.

It is stated in *Slugg's Manchester Fifty Years Ago*, p. 309,
that the races which form the subject of this letter, after
being set on foot, were kept up for fifteen years, and then
discontinued; but that, in another fifteen years, they were
reestablished, after which they were held annually at
Whitsuntide on Kersal Moor until 1846, when the locality
was changed. 'On the second attempt, though a very
long and severe paper war was carried on against their
renewal, they retained their hold upon the public, and in 1777
the grand stand was built . . . . Unlike the present race-
course, as I am told, the moor was as free as the air you
breathe there. Under the stands were drinking-bars, which
were let off to various publicans.' (A placard announcing
races in September 1760 is cited in *Remains*, vol. ii, part i,
p. 305, *note*.)

Whether or not the personal circumstances in which the
following lines were composed involved something beyond
what we are either able or eager to conjecture, it is impossible
to mistake the lofty as well as gentle spirit of the writer; though
at the same time we may regret that the homily should have

been so long drawn out as to lose something of its force. The concluding passages of the epistle are in some respects obscure; but this cannot be helped.]

DEAR Son of Darcy, for a Father's sake
    I wish your ardent mind would be awake
To something worthier of the Pedigree
Than this Horse-racing Stewardship can be;
Some nobler theme for you to judge upon
Than 'Hey! they come, they come! They're gone, they're
    gone!'
From your good-natur'd Temper one expects,
And gen'rous turn, more similar Effects
Than Invitations to commence a Rout
That tends to bring disturbances about;   10
Which, if blameworthy in the vulgar crew,
Can by no means be laudable in you,
Whom Heav'n has made the Steward of a Mind,
Body, Estate, for other Scenes design'd,
And, with a watchful Eye, preserv'd thro' all
The Scenes that—Gratitude will but recall,
And prompt the Use and End of Thought, of Health,
Of, unacquir'd by your own Labour, Wealth.
In some poor Cote had you receiv'd [your] birth,
Been forc'd to dig the Alkringtonian earth,   20
Or make the Brick for the high-mounted Dome
Which now is your hereditary Home,

19. *Transcript : a birth.*

9. *Rout:* gathering or assembly.
19. *Cote,* cot.
20. Cf. Baines's *Lancashire,* ed. Croston, vol. ii, pp. 351-3: 'Alkrington Hall, a substantial red brick mansion with stone dressings, erected in the early part of the last [eighteenth] century, stands upon elevated ground in the midst of picturesque woods overlooking Heaton Park, but the surroundings have of late years been sadly marred by the close proximity of the cotton mills and chemical works of Middleton.'

Or weave the Dress in which you are array'd,
Slave to the Loom, the Trowel, or the Spade;
Had you e'er felt the hardships which the Poor,
To make their Neighbours 'Gentlemen' endure:
For other Judgment would your feeling Soul
Conceive of Station at a Starting Pole?
You would not think of Brute-huzzaing Shout,
But human Blessings, all the year about—   30
Of Charity, a Premium better sure
Than Oath and Curse and Riot on a Moor!
To make that kind of Stewardship a choice,
Your better Genius cannot give the Voice;
The gentle Whisper of your inner Sense
Must be o'ercome by clamorous Pretence.
In Justice to it, let the calmer hour
Permit your Reason to exert its Power,
To paint in its true Colours all the scene
Of Dissolution that expects a reign   40
From your Encouragement to take its course,
And, as the case now seems to stand, by Force—
A shocking Circumstance! And if, unsure
Of legal Right, you will command the Moor,
You, whose Resentment was so lately shown
In case of Fishpond Property—your own—
Will bear the blame of such an ugly job
As can succeed by nothing but a Mob.
Evil-disposèd Persons may abscond,
Yet steal the Fish of Ashton Lever's Pond,   50
And, tho' Severity should advertize
Its utmost Prosecution, gain their Prize.
But Ashton Lever cannot well invade
His Neighbour's land, to make a Cavalcade,

27. *For other Judgment.* Instead of a different judicial office.

45. *Fishpond Property.* Of these fishponds no trace appears to remain; nor is it likely that anything is known as to the poaching in them.

Or sale of liquors, and the mobbing sort,
Not Fish, about him, for their kind of sport!
  Give me, dear Son of my deceasèd Friend,
To know what Obligation, or what End,
You have or would propose in this affair,
Which hurries on, to chain you to a Chair,   60
For which you risk, for any trifling fame,
The chance of being horridly to blame,
For treating Neighbours upon either side
In such a sort as—*You* would scarce abide.
  The printed Call to come again and Dine,
And toss your Rights amidst the circling Wine
The Freedoms, heighten'd by reputed Fame,
Would all be wrong, if *Lever* was the name;
Nor can the name of Gentleman avail
Without inferior help amidst its Ale,   70
Where humbler votaries may take the hint
Of such Conventions as you cannot stint.
  Like to become, so far as I have learn'd,
A party (I may truly say) concern'd,
I seek the way that may the least offend
One whom I wish all Blessings to attend,
To represent it as not worth his while
Thus to continue advertizing style.
The chance—the hope—of less'ning all offence
Urges Appeal to his reflecting Sense: 80
Whether, supposing him to force a Race
Against, at least, *one* Owner of the Place,
The fetching a few horses from afar
Will make amends for the domestic jar,
For the uneasiness (if heart of steel
Be not the case) that he himself must feel,

55. *Sale of liquors.* See *introductory note.* The ' printed Call ' in l. 65 seems to refer to some advertisement of refreshments issued with the authority of the Stewards.

60. *Chair,* office (the stewardship of the races).

And friends and families—the dreaded fruit,
Amongst them all, of such a fond pursuit?
  This Race of life, a little longer run,
May show some things which might have not been done,   90
And he no worse—this would, I think, be one,
Which I entreat him to reflect upon.
If he refuses—if a Steward's name
Has got the most authoritative claim—
Of *three* Proprietors, if one, alone,
Consent of *two* suffices to postpone;
From grieving Friends he cannot take it ill,
If, to prevent the progress of ill-will,
In Town or Country, Strangers or Allied,
They wish its Cause might soon be laid aside.   100

A 'RESERVED' ADDRESS,

[Although the following poetical epistle concerning a 'reserved' rather than 'rejected' address may exemplify the saw *'facit indignatio versus,'* it assuredly makes a great pother about a trivial cause. It possesses, however, a certain local as well as personal interest, inasmuch as it connects itself directly with the series of *Verses spoken at the Breaking-up of the Free Grammar School in Manchester*, printed in vol. i, pp. 148–177, as well as with the piece following upon them.

Internal evidence, which has been pointed out to me by Mr. C. W. Sutton, proves that these lines, addressed by Byrom to an unknown correspondent, clearly an intimate friend and possibly a Feoffee of the School like himself, were written in the earlier part of the high-mastership of the Rev. William Purnall, or Purnell, which lasted from 1749 to 1764. John Arden, the 'J. Arden' mentioned in l. 4, is shown by the School Register (vol. i, p. 54) to have entered the School, together with his brother, Richard Pepper Arden (afterwards the first Lord Alvanley) in June 1752. They were both sons of John Arden, afterwards of Harden, who was born in 1709 (cf. *Remains*, vol. ii, p. 503, *note*). The 'Martin' of l. 5 must have been Samuel, son of the Rev. Samuel Martin of Gotham, Notts, and previously Master of Appleby School, Leicestershire; he entered Manchester Grammar School, according to the Register (vol. i, p. 58), in September 1754. His father (?), Dr. Martin, was an early intimate of Byrom's (cf. *Remains*, vol. i, p. 335, *et al*). William Purnall, who was of Oriel College, Oxford, was appointed Second Master in 1723, and held this office during the last three years of J. Richards' and during the whole of Henry Brooke's high-mastership (1727—1749), and then himself succeeded to the 'archididuscation' dignity. To him

E

seems due the fact that the School was not wholly ruined
during the rule of the last two High Masters. (See R. D.
Hodgson, *A Short History of the Manchester Grammar
School*, p. 30.) Cf. as to Purnall, *ante*, vol. i, p. 250, and
Remains, vol. ii, p. 502, *note*.]

I may perhaps mention that a MS. presented to the
Manchester Grammar School Library by Mrs. Finch Smith,
the widow of Prebendary Finch Smith, on March 19th, 1897,
which consists of a collection of Latin verses spoken at the
Grammar School on the occasion of the birth, in 1640, of
Prince Henry, third son of King Charles I and afterwards
Duke of Gloucester, contains some hexameters and distichs
by 'Edmund Byrom'—doubtless the youngest son of Adam
Byrom of the Salford Branch, who was baptised at the
Collegiate Church, Manchester, in 1623, and died unmarried.]

I.

WHAT can sudden Reflection conceive of this Letter:
    'Much pleas'd with your Fable?' Well, so much the
        better :
Then it answers the Purpose for which it was meant.
'And have ordered J. Arden to speak it.' Content !
'Your verses for Martin he'll drop for this year,
And reserve, with your leave, for another.' Hold there !
That Lad has been tried, and has done very well;
How another may answer, one cannot foretell.

II.

If you see any Reasons so fair and so fit
As to ask a Reserve, I shall freely submit;   10
But the two that you mention, I cannot but think,
Must appear, at first Reading, unworthy of Ink :
For, when all had been done, to comply with request,
And the verses adjusted, the Lad, and the rest—
'A Lad to repeat them *he* cannot well spare,'
Is a Reason to me neither fitting nor fair.

   4, 5. See *introductory note*.

III.

For, had it been either, 'twas sure to occur,
When we met at your House and made the Demur,
As the Lads unprovided were Jackson and Martin,
And no Exercise giv'n 'em to have any Part in,
Mr. Purnall might chuse which he would of the two,
Tho' Martin was thought full as proper by you,   20
Having had the like Task; so the Point was agreed,
And now *'not to spare'* is not right in good Deed.

IV.

So that Reason the first for 'not sparing' a Lad,
As it stands by itself, is apparently bad.
If a better come forth, I have nothing to say;
But the second is made of no finer Clay:
Viz., 'the sameness of Task both for Martin and Arden';
Tho', excepting their growth in the sameness of Garden,
For the sake of Repenting, for Stanza, for Metre,
Variation, in Verse, could not well be completer.   30

V.

And Verse was your choice. But, however, with these,
If a sameness displeases, dispense, if you please.
But I cannot consent, with my Paper and Pen,
That *The Ape and the Fox* should demolish the Men;
Nor would I usurp the Headmaster's own Right
As to Verses or Proses, or Lad to recite;
But, whilst I contend, with poetical nerve,
To comply with Request, I object to—Reserve.

17. Mr. Sutton suggests that this may possibly have been Cyril Jackson (afterwards Dean of Christ Church), who was admitted to the school in 1755. (*School Register,* vol. i, p. 62.)

19. See *introductory note.*

34. For *The Ape and the Fox* see vol. i, pp. 160-2, *ante.* Which tale or fable is here called *'* The Men,' can hardly be decided; it may be one which has not come down to us.

VI.

Last year, to oblige him, came Verse on the Comet,
And, at his Innuendo, went instantly from it   40
To the choice which he made of *The Three Crows, a Tale;*
And a Lad was then 'spared' to conclude the regale.
For his Master judg'd right, that, at Breaking-up Time,
Some cheerfuller English, in Prose or in Rhime,
Would please the Folks best; and, according to Rumour,
The Session broke up in a very good Humour.

VII.

And this, I suppose, made the Spectacle Verse
To come into his mind, for Lad to rehearse;
As you mention'd to me, when you sup'd in my Room,
That night when the Fire happen'd—you and young
        Hulme—   50
And, but for that accident, said your Intent
Was a Message next Day, to obtain a Consent;
As the Season drew nigh, and the time was but short,
He wanted, you told me, some Rhimes of that Sort.

VIII.

The Spectatcle Story containing too few,
I thought of uniting another thereto,
And [pieced] them together, as well as I could,
Leaving all to the Master, to do what he would.
You settled the Bus'ness, but still had a mind

57. Transcript : placed. Pieced, conj.

39. *Verse on the Comet.* Apparently non-extant.

41. For *The Three Black Crows, a Tale,* see vol. i, pp. 151-5.

47. *The Spectacle Verse.* This, again, it is impossible to identify.

50. In the appalling list of Manchester fires given in Axon's *Annals of Manchester,* there seems to be none early enough to suit the probable date of the poem.—A Thomas Hulme occurs as Borough-reeve of Salford in 1746 (*ib.,* p. xiii.).

Of a Piece for J. Arden, of Metrical Kind, 60
Which I found, upon searching, had made its Escape;
So I sent, in the Room on't, *The Fox and the Ape.*

IX.

And, along with that Paper, the other was sent,
With addition and change, in the Manner you meant—
Your Answer, expressing full End of my Task,
And that both should be sent to the *Archididasc.*
Would not, therefore, a Letter, which Arden the younger,
Brings, after all this, puzzle any Guessmonger;
With 'Reserve, by your Leave,' so concisely declared,
'For another year's Reckoning—Lad cannot be spared.' 70

X.

'Such a Lad as the Master could wish,' you have added.
Now, pray, by whose wish were the Verses unladded?
For they had one by his, and by yours, and by mine,
If assent, without scruple, may pass for a sign.
Has the Lad any wishes himself in the case,
Or objection to speaking? Then, let it take place;
Or, if anything else is (not mentioned) amiss,
Be so free as to tell me what really it is!

XI.

Have you got, unexpectedly, such a Supply
As you think would do better? Why, then, so do I; 80
You gave about Verses so tardy an Item,
And I made so much Haste, in Compliance to write 'em,

66. The High Master; to whom, it thus appears, the present verses were not directly addressed.

72. *Unladded.* Deprived of a lad to speak them.

76. *Take place.* Cf. Byrom's awkward use of this phrase, in a much more important collocation, in *Christians, awake,* v. 42 (*ante,* vol. ii, p. 22).

77. *Not mentioned.* Without being mentioned.

To patch 'em, and piece 'em, and turn 'em about,
That Friends may have sent you some better, no doubt;
If they have, do but say so, and all will be right;
But such Logic as this is not over-polite.

XII.

Till then—as the Proof of a Pudding is Eating,
And the Sause to give Verses a Relish, Repeating—
If the Lad be not 'spar'd' whose Repeating was tried,
By one that yet is not mine dare not abide.   90
Pray send 'em both back, to the Muse that must own 'em
She herself can receive them for Horace's *Nonum*,
And wish, without Fear of 'unsparing' Disaster,
Success to the Lads, and their honest Head Master.

87. 'There is,' says another proverb, 'no deceit in a bag pudding.'

92. Hor. *Ars Poetica*, vv. 388-9 :

*Nonumque prematur in annum
Membranis intus positis.*

THE BELLY AND THE LIMBS.

[A note by Canon Raines states that this piece is ' an allegory taken from Menenius Philodemus, c. 9, sect. 15.' What or who can be here meant? Not Philodemus of Gadara, in whose fragments found at Herculaneum nothing of the kind occurs, though he might well have illustrated his discussion of the art of rhetoric by the story. On the other hand, ' Philodemus ' seems suggestive of some ' Poplicola ' unknown. The fable related by Menenius Agrippa in Plutarch (*Coriolanus*, c. 6) with its application to the relations between the Senate and the people at Rome, is translated by A. W. Verity in his Cambridge University Press edition of Shakespeare's *Coriolanus*, where the two versions can be conveniently compared. Mr. Verity points out how all that Plutarch says of Menenius Agrippa is that he was ' chief man of the embassy of the pleasantest old men and the most acceptable to the people,' sent by the Senate to remonstrate with them after their secession, and that the character in the play 'represents a sort of inference from Plutarch's words ("the pleasantest old men") and from the style of reasoning Menenius addressed to the people.'

Byrom, *more suo*, has elaborated the apologue, but not unskilfully.]

I.

THE Limbs complain'd, as ancient story goes,
　For want of food, from Shoulders down to Toes:
How hard they, all of 'em, were forc'd to work,
And how the Belly us'd 'em like a Turk,
Grown, by their Labour, fat itself and plump,
Neglected Limbs, and sat upon the Rump.

II.

Some Hands drew for 'em an Address, 'tis said,
And laid their Grievances before the Head;
In threat'ning Terms, for due Relief applied;
Nam'd what it was, and would not be denied.　　　10
Good subjects they; but not so far befool'd
As to submit, if Tyrant Belly rul'd.

III.

The Head look'd at 'em with compassion, too;
As, in such Case, all Heads of sense would do.
Head knew that Belly, fatt'ning more than meet,
Made work much harder, both for Hands and Feet,
And gave, besides, proportionable Pain
To the Purveyor for 'em all—the Brain.

7. The 'address' in writing is an addition, appropriate to a parliamentary age, which would not have occurred to Shake-speare.

IV.

'Dear Limbs,' said he, 'Im sorry for your sake;
Whene'er you suffer, I am sure to ake.   20
My Mouth is open for your just Defence;
But, pray, consider, with your common sense,
Were it not so for Belly's Income, too,
Nor Bit nor Sup could ever reach to you.

V.

'From bad to worse will things go on, of course,
Against the Belly if you bend your force;
For, fill'd with more than is enough, or less,
You draw from thence the Strength that you possess.
Both of you want each other's Help, and should,
For mutual Safety, seek each other's Good.   30

VI.

What can a Head, united by the Ties
Of Nature, Sirs, to all of you, devise?
Amidst a Tumult, I should do my best,
Not without Hopes of seeing Ills redrest;
But your Excesses tend to lay me flat—
And what will any of you get by that?

VII.

Pray, be compos'd, and shun the wild extreme,
That Thought may form some salutary Scheme
For due Relief, as this is the Design
Of Understanding! Limbs and Belly join,   40
And, whilst the Head is seeking Wisdom's Part,
Go, and consult the Goodness of the Heart!

THE PERILS OF HUNTER'S CROFT.

[Mr. Battersbee or Battersby, to whom this playful epistle is addressed, was a Manchester friend of Byrom's, and a scholar of his Shorthand Club (cf. *Remains*, vol. i, p. 315). He was probably the Thomas Battersbee who was Borough-reeve of Manchester 1761–2 (Axon, *Annals of Manchester*, p. xi), and doubtless before this a person of consequence in the town.

These lilting stanzas have considerable local interest. Hunter's Croft, Hunter's Lane (now called Cannon Street), ran on the south side of it into Hanging Ditch, near the corner of which stood Byrom's house. (See J. T. Slugg, *Reminiscences of Manchester Fifty Years Ago* (1881), pp. 128–9.) In February 1739, Byrom addresses a letter to his wife as residing 'near the Great Church' (the present Cathedral) in Manchester. *Remains*, vol. ii, p. 219. In the later years of his life, he lived in Fennell Street. (Cf. *ante*, p. 9, *introductory note* to *A Letter to His Wife at Kersal.*)]

I.

DEAR Brother Battersbee, a Case
   Lies here so plain before my Face—
Where people are beheld, full oft,
Passing along thro' Hunter's Croft,
Both to and from the Market Cross—
That I am really at a Loss
How to reply to them that hint
The Danger visible that's in't.

4. For a description of the Old Market Place and neighbouring streets in 1772 see *Manchester Collectanea* (Chetham Society), vol. ii, pp. 209 *sqq.* Mr. Harland speaks of the Old Market Cross, ' with the stocks, pillory, well-named the tea-table, upon which I have seen them dwell, when whipped by the beadle. Now we are at the Short Millgate again.'

II.

Danger, I am reduc'd to say,
Can be but little in the Day;   10
And, at this time o' th' year, the night
Yields a sufficient Share of Light,
To show how Track, that Feet went o'er
So diametrical before,
Is turn'd to Angle, not to Sides,
That now must regulate their Strides.

III.

Your Mathematics, Sir, they cry,
May possibly escape an eye
More elevated tow'rds the Pole,
Of some unsuspecting Soul   20
In wonted Progress, led to think
On something else than unknown Brink,
Whose foot, betray'd into the Gap,
May bring his Head to dire mishap.

IV.

'What, in the Daytime?' Why, between
That corner there without a Screen,
Turn is so sudden, and so short,
That Foot, prepar'd by custom for 't,
May, by an usual step, be caught,
Before the Brain can tell its thought;   30
Which, though it might have seen the spot,
It may so chance that it may not.

V.

Then, in the Night, Cloud, Rain, or Shade,
May so obscure the ambuscade
That careless child, or man that's drunk,
May not, so soon, see Cellar sunk.

But, to cut short the gen'ral strain,
Of all observers who complain,
I'll only note, upon this Head,
What one, who quoted Moses, said. . .   40

VI.

'In building a new House,' said he,
'Moses enjoined a Jew to see
That, by a Fall from where he stood
No Man might bring upon it Blood,
To make a Battlement at Top.
Now, lest unwary Christian drop,
Before this House is built, I trow,
Here wants a Battlement below.'

VII.

The man, tho' grave, pursued th' affair
With a good-natur'd, friendly air,   50
And talk'd how little Cost would do
For setting up a Rail or two,
Of strength enough to make mischance
Forbear its dangerous advance.
'A word to Battersbee,' he ended,
'And Case, I'll answer for 't, is mended.'

VIII.

Now, lest the Leg, or Neck, or Arm,
Of any Soul should come to Harm :
If Front of Danger does not soon
Wear some admonishing Pompoon,   60
By the first Rhimes that can be prest
I send you notice for the Rest :   )
'Safe be the House, and ev'ry Guest }
That ever it shall harbour Blest !   )

41 *sqq.* See *Deuteronomy*, ch. xxii, v. 8 : ' When thou buildest a new house; then thou shalt make a battlement for thy roof, that thou bring not blood upon thine house, if any man fall from thence.'

60. *Pompoon*, French *pompon*, top-knot worn by women on the forehead.

THE GRAMMAR SCHOOL MILLS.

[Some account of the history of the celebrated Grammar School Mills upon the Irk will be found in the introductory note to Byrom's epigram *Bone and Skin*, vol. i, pp. 109-10, *ante* (as to which see, also, *Addenda et Corrigenda* in *Appendix II* below). This may be supplemented from the very clear narrative of the history of the mills, which originally comprised a corn mill, a malt mill and a fulling mill, in Mr. R. D. Hodgson's *Short History of the Manchester Grammar School*, pp. 16–20). It there appears that the law-suits arising out of attempts to infringe the oppressive monopoly of the Grammar School Mills began as early as forty years after the foundation of the School, and in the end amounted to threescore, without the suppression of the offence of 'grinding away'—*i.e.*, elsewhere than at the School Mills—having been brought about. The Act of 1758 put an end to the monopoly of the Mills as to the grinding of corn, but left it untouched as to malt fixing the charge at a shilling for six bushels. (See the statement cited from Whatton's *History of Manchester* in *Remains*, vol. i, p. 319 note.) At first, the new condition of things acted favourably upon the revenue of the School from the Mills; but, in course of time, the struggle began again with regard to the grinding of malt, and, so late as 1856, a deputation of brewers complained stating that the fixed charge was excessive in the ratio of three to one. (The fact that, to this day, the great breweries of Manchester lie outside the township is noticeable in this connexion.) The rights of the Malt Mill, it would appear, never came to any definite termination. The last payment was received in 1858. When the Lancashire and Yorkshire Railway established its station in the midst of the School property, and paid a chief rent amounting to something like £2500, a solution of the Feoffees' difficulty had at last been found; for the profits from the Mills had long sunk from twice that sum, a figure which they had reached about the close of the eighteenth century.

In the times of scarcity, which came to a head at Manchester, in November 1757, with a serious riot at Shudehill, and the destruction of a corn mill at Clayton (cf. a full account of this affair in *Transactions of the Lancashire and Cheshire Antiquarian Society*, vol. xxviii, pp. 87 *sqq*), Byrom's feeling seems to have been against the monopoly—or at all events against two of the lessees who had to make their profits under it; but when, in the following year, a direct remedy was sought by legislation, he inevitably, as a Feoffee of the Grammar School, perceived a ' divided duty ' arising out of the situation which he very frankly describes in the lines following.]

I.

D EAR Sirs,
              It is true that I am Feoffee
For the Mills of the School; but your asking of me
What Scheme the Petitioners have in their view,
Is applying to one as much puzzl'd as you.
They themselves, I am told, are not fully agreed
Except in one point, and that is, *To succeed;*
But how—in what Matter, or Manner or Mill—
That Reck'ning must come when they bring in their Bill.

II.

For the Good of the Town, they would have us convey
What we cannot, perhaps, so well manage as they—   10
The Mills, and the Lands appertaining thereto.
Now, this, at first sight, one cannot well do;
For, in Persons maintaining a Charity Trust,
Such a sudden Compliance would hardly be just;
Tho' I wish, for my part, if the Good of the Town
Would rise up in their room, that the Mills were all down.

9. *Convey,* execute a convey-
ance of transfer.

III.

But, there is the Question—and what for the good
Of both County and Town, should be well understood.
For, altho', in a custom continued so long,
There may, without Wonder, be somewhat that's wrong, 20
Yet a Parliament Bill should be weigh'd a bit longer,
Lest the Town should be saddl'd with somewhat that's
          wronger;
Lest the Grant of new Pow'rs to a new Set of Folks
Should subject the Town to more ponderous Yokes.

IV.

Its Lands or its Houses, its Windows and Lights
Pay nothing, at present, to day Mill Rights;
Nor has A, B, or C any Levy [to] raise,
Distrain and Distress, in the Gentleman's Phrase—
Some Gentleman's Phrase; for indeed other some
Were against this attempt, and the Major Part dumb;   30
So that no Disagreement, as yet, can I see
Betwixt the good Town and her loving Feoffee.

V.

And the End of a Suit, on which Damage depended,
Which, if some did not hinder, would quickly be ended?
We were willing to lease, by our Answer appears,
All the Mills that we hold, for the term of ten years
(And we could not for more), if the Town would accept
Of the choice of Lessees, and the Custom be kept.
Now, let some, one and all, put themselves in our Place,
And inform us what more could be said in such Case?   40

VI.

We gave to the Question concerning Expense,
Some Gentlemen thought, satisfactory Sense
To prevent, in all cases of Grinding or Flour,
Both abuse of School Rights and abuse of School Power;

Intent on performing, as well as we could,
A Particular Trust for the General Good.
And no Gentleman need to be so [much] disgusted;
For with Breaking the Custom we are not entrusted.

VII.

That the Suit may go on, and the Parliament too,
And about the same Point, is a Method quite new.　　50
But how a Feoffee can consent to the Bill,
While he sues for the Custom, surpasses my skill.
They would think him, I doubt, either foolish or mad,
Both to hold it for good and to drop it for bad;
And the School might be suing, tho' Losses were great—
Short Line of Discernment may fathom that Feat.

VIII.

They object Insufficiency to a poor Mill,
That for want of its Grist is obliged to stand still
By the Dealers and Millers, who, after one Day,
If it were not ground fór them, might grind it away;　　60
And, in case of some Chance, if the A's and the B's
Can prevent other grinding, when They are Trustees,
As Proposal has told us—if no other aim
Be design'd in its Make—cannot we do the same?

IX.

As concerning the Building of which you have spoken,
That will soon be set up when the Custom is broken.
For the grinding of Wheat in vast quantities down,
I know nothing on't but from Vulgar renown;

49. That the suit at law may be carried on by the persons who are promoting the Bill in Parliament.

56. It does not need much discernment to perceive such a piece of folly.

63-4. If the proposal is made *bonâ fide,* cannot wĕ School Feoffees find other grinders as easily as the new Trustees could, to whom we are asked to transfer the Mills?

67. *For,* as to.
68. *Renown,* report.

Nor have had curiosity in me for poring
Where the Man that you hint at has been at his boring. 70
But I wish that all Change, in the matter of Mills,
May have less or not greater than *Charity Ills*.

X.

One would not suppose that, to make a Bill pass,
Any persons conceal any Snake in the Grass.
I respect all the Gentlemen, some and some other,
Tho' lamenting, for Both, Disagreéable Pother,
And expense of the Rich, that were better bestow'd
Upon such as now feel a more sensible Load;
Nor can I conceive, how a Parliament rout
Should produce greater good than fair Methods without. 80

XI.

We Feoffees have the Trouble; the School has the Gains—
Of what Use is reproach for our well-meaning Pains?
Notwithstanding Defects, let the Alphabet doubt
Whether College, or Church, be entirely without,
And propose it to them, that Rotation of Letter
May take their Belongings and manage them better;
For I think, without vying with College or Chapter,
The proposal, to us, not a Syllable apter.

70. The meaning of this is obscure. To *bore* may be used in the sense of 'to push forward.'

72. *Charity Ills* seems to mean the evils attendant upon the administration of a charity (which, certainly, are so great and frequent as to deserve a specific designation).

75. *Some and some other,* All and sundry.

76. *Both.* Obscure.

79. *Parliament rout,* the trouble of a parliamentary campaign (not the defeat of a bill in Parliament).

83-6. One must suppose that there was a proposal for a nomination of trustees according to some alphabetical order of sequence. Byrom asks whether this principle might not, with equal aptitude or ineptitude, be applied to the management of the property of the Collegiate Church.

XII.

If the Parliament does, we must yield to our Betters :
There are some, to be sure, amongst men of all Letters; 90
And it's well if some worse, from the A's to the uzzards,
Do not make the Town wish for their countryfied Buzzards.
But, when I reflect how the Workhouse and Cut,
Tho' they both were so good, being hasty of foot,
Miscarried, by leaving Agreement behind,
I expect a Third Instance of Similar Kind.

91. The ' uzzards ' must mean the z's; but, though an uncomplimentary epithet has been attached to that letter, the present designation of it remains unintelligible. A 'buzzard' is a dunce.

93. As to the workhouse, see *introductory note* to *A Manchester Memorandum, ante*, p. 26. The allusion to the ' cut ' is obscure; it probably refers to some contemplated street improvement.

A THOUGHT STOLEN FROM CATO.

[A long search for the 'thought' Byrom professes to have 'stolen from Cato' has proved fruitless, although it has extended through what remains from the hand of the elder Cato, as well as the praises of old age which Cicero puts into the mouth of Cato Uticensis, and which here and there approach rather near to the sentiment on which Byrom's lines are based. The distichs *de Moribus* of Dionysius Cato have also been gone through in vain for the same purpose, as well as Addison's tragedy (although this was a production which Byrom greatly disliked; see *ante*, vol. i, p. 218), besides the ' Essays on liberty, civil and religious, and other important subjects' which, under the title of *Cato's Letters*, reached their sixth edition in 1755. A query kindly admitted into *Notes and Queries* also failed to elicit a reply.]

F

VICE may give pleasure, Virtue may give pain.
   True; but how long will such a Truth remain?
The moment only, while the Actions last;
'Tis false, as soon as ever they are past.
Then pleasure vanishes, which Vice had brought,
And in its room comes ever painful thought;
Then Pain is gone, which Virtue had endur'd,
And Pleasure comes, eternally secur'd.

UPON MADAME ANTOINETTE BOURIGNON.

WRIT TO MRS. PHEBE BYROM.

[Concerning (Mlle.) Antoinette Bourignon, and Byrom's
reverence for her writings (she died in 1680) see *ante*, vol. ii,
pp. 65-7; and cf. notes to the *Verses* printed after these.   See
also Dr. A. R. MacEwen's *Antoinette Bourignon, Quietist*
(1910), where it is mentioned that, in 1739, notwithstanding
the remonstrances of Byrom, who feared that offence might be
caused, two of her hymns were included by John and Charles
Wesley in their *Collection of Psalms and Hymns.*—As to
' Sister Phebe ' cf. *introductory note* to the lines *To Mrs.
Phebe Byrom*, ante, p. 6].

THERE was an innocent and holy Maid,
   That lov'd poor Folks, wept, fasted, watch'd and pray'd:
'O Lord, take Pity on my tender Youth;
All Men are Liars—do Thou teach me Truth!'
God heard her Prayers, and was Himself her Guide,
And she knew more than all the World beside.

VERSES OCCASION'D BY THE PREFACE TO A BOOK ENTITULED THE SNAKE IN THE GRASS, etc..

[The reader has just been referred to the lines headed *Leslie v. Bourignon* in vol. ii, *ante*; and Appendix v to the same volume contains a solemn travesty by Byrom of the substantial part of the Preface to Leslie's *Snake in the Grass*, where Antoinette Bourignon is held up to reprobation. For a general account of Charles Leslie's position and prowess see Sir Leslie Stephen's *History of English Thought in the Eighteenth Century*, vol. i (2nd edn.), pp. 194 *sqq*; Leslie, who is there said to have been pronounced by Johnson 'the only non-juror who could reason,' is described as having, 'besides numerous skirmishes' found time to carry on operations against Quakers, Deists, Socinians, Jews and Papists.' *The Snake in the Grass; or Satan Transformed into an Angel of Light* (1696) (Leslie, as a born controversialist, knew the value of drastic titles) was openly directed against 'the Deep and Unsuspected *Subtilty* which is Couched under the Pretended *Simplicity*,' of 'many of the *Principal Leaders* of Those People call'd Quakers,' and strove to display 'the frightful and stupendous Prospect of *Quakerism*' as a warning against 'other sorts of *Enthusiasm*, that seem more Plausible; but spring all from the same Stock; and draw after them the same Damnable Consequence.' To Byrom the ruthless uncharitableness of this self-confident champion was not more repugnant than was the gross unfairness of the personal application of his relentless parable to a woman whom he charged with a 'Pharisaical show of Piety,' while Byrom regarded her as one of the saints of God.

After the appearance of the second edition of *The Snake in the Grass* an answer to it was published by the eminent

quaker George Whitehead (who was largely instrumental in
bringing about the passing of the Act of Toleration in 1689)
under the title of *An Antidote against the Venome of the
Snake in the Grass* (1697), with a *Supplement* (1699) in answer
to a reply under the same title added by Leslie to his third
edition.   Whitehead's title corresponds to the definition of
'Snakes in the grass' given in the 'Remarks' prefixed to a
farce of that name by J. B. Buckstone in Cumberland's
British Theatre, vol. xxiv: 'Those who, under the guises
and pretence, make the most insidious designs, whose exterior
is mild and conciliatory, but whose breath is venom and
poison.'   Aaron Hill's *The Snake in the Grass*, posthumously
printed in his *Works* (1760), is said by Genest (vol. x, p. 180)
to be 'a tolerable Satire on Pantomimes and Operas.'   The
phrase is due to Verg. *Ecl.* iii, v. 93 : *'latet anguis in herba.'*]

W HAT an exceedingly severe Opinion
    Is here pronounced against the Maid Bourignon,
Who has no Share, at all, in the Debates
To which the Book, thus introduced, relates—
No more to do with 'Snakes' in any 'Grass'
Than a poor Sheep that fed upon it has !
    Tho' all were true that better books prefer
Against the Quakers, what is that to her ?
She was no Quaker; she profest the Claim

7. Byrom's opinion of Quakers
and Quakerism is summarised in
his letter to Ephraim Lampe
cited *ante,* vol. ii, appendix v,
p. 593.

8. Mlle. Bourignon's *A Warning against Quakers* was published in an English translation
in 1708.

9. Mlle. Bourignon began to
publish at her private press in
1668.   The Quakers may be said
to have " had a name," at all

events from the date of the
Quaker Act (1662).   In 1660,
at Lancaster Castle, George Fox,
in reply to the charge that he
was 'a cheife upholder of the
Quakers sect ' stated that ' the
Quakers are not a sect, but were
in the power of god before sects
was, and wittnes the election
before the world began.' " (*The
Journal of George Fox* (ed. 1911),
vol. i, p. 379.)

To inward Light, before they had a name.   10
Furly, a chief amongst the rising Sect,
Published a Book against her, to detect
(He said) the Spirit which she acted by
And had his own discover'd, in Reply.
It is a Calumny, beyond a doubt,
Against all sense and reason to cry out :
'She and the Quakers perfectly agree :
They run the Priesthood down, and so does she.'
By what her Quaker adversary penn'd,
She was to Priests and Sacraments a Friend ;   20
By what the Preface would attempt to show,
She was to Priests and Sacrament a Foe.'
Whether she was, or whether she was not.
On either side she has the same hard lot—
The lot, full oft, of generous Respect
To Truths, as such, without Regard to Sect.
'Tis plain, however, in this Case, to see
That witnesses against her don't agree ;
Nor can a stronger instance well be shown
Of Sentence pass'd from Prejudice alone   30
Than such as make her Writings to admit
The very Maxims against which she writ :
She writ—and her Accuser owns it, too—
Concerning the Respect to Pastors due,
Against the Quakers—what a just Appeal
There lies against such a remorseless zeal,
Not in this point alone, but all the rest,
Altho', perhaps, more plausibly exprest !
For, if the Main Desire to bring her in,
And stile her Cousin of the Quaker Kin,   40
Be so absurd that her pretended Crime

---

11. Benjamin Furly, a friend and fellow-traveller of William Penn, and afterwards a correspondent of Locke, published, in Dutch, *Anthoinette Bourignon ontdeckt ende haeren Geest geopenbart* (Amsterdam, 1671).

Is urg'd and answer'd at the selfsame Time,
What thinking Reader will, without suspense
Till he examines, take the rigid Sense
Impos'd on broken sentences and pickt,
Which whole ones, possibly, may contradict?
And other Passages, with greater ease,
Clear up the cloudy Comment upon these,
Retail'd, along the prefatory Page,
With such a semblance of unguarded Rage   50
As (to apply the borrow'd Terms) appears
'Abhorrent, utterly, to Christian Ears;
Where you will find no Charity display'd,
No humble Thought, no kind Allowance made
Of fair Construction of another's good,
That may, so construed, soon be understood,
No love, no Condescension,' and so on—
Things which the Prefacer, when thought upon,
With all his Eloquence might well commend,
But hardly practise, whilst the cruel End   60
Of Commendation was but to infer
That—these the Devil could not teach to Her.
From him, 'tis said her Inspirations come,
And that her *Witchcraft* has deluded some
Possess'd of Sense and Learning—some abroad,
And some at home, defend her and applaud.
What Haste for Devilry forbids to stay
And hear what some—some one at least—may say:
Poiret, for instance, whom one Leaf has phras'd
A Man of Sense—and actually craz'd: 70
Craz'd in one Page, and of a crazy Fame,
Tho', to support it, not a single name;
Plac'd, in the next, among the Men of Sense,
Who, when deluded, writ in her Defence?
Such Inconsistences does Hate pursue,

62. This sentence is thirty-two lines in length!

Both with respect to her and Poiret, too—
A man of Heart and Head, sincere and sound
Lover of Truth, wherever it was found.
Of useful Volumes be increas'd the Store,
Writer of many, Publisher of more,   80
That show his Worth—and Reason's utter Want
In 'Mad Disciple,' 'Devil of a Saint.'
Strange Language this! If 'Devil' she had been,
The searching Poiret would have seen, wherein;
Who judg'd, from what he saw himself, and knew,
God's Inspiration of her to be true,
And not the Devil's. From that Source was had
The Jew Reproach : 'A Devil' and 'is mad'—
By human Frailty borrow'd, to upbraid
The honest Witness, and the guiltless Maid.   90
Her Works are extant, some in English, too:
Let the fair Judge, who is inclin'd to view,
Without surrend'ring to an open Foe,
For mangled Bits and Scraps, his Ay and No,
See for himself in such an equal Light
As would be pleaded for, were he to write,
Setting aside all controversial Fray,
Or what the Sect that he is of may say,
And, well consider'd, form his own opinion
From her own Writings, of the Maid Bourignon!   100

76. For Byrom's opinion of Pierre Poiret, who edited the works of Antoinette Bourignon in 19 vols. (Amsterdam, 1679 sqq.), with a Life in 2 (ib. 1683) see *Remains*, vol. ii, pp. 216-7 : He ' was, I thought, an honest man and very clever, but his mistress was an original, which he was not,' etc.

82. Cf. Preface (p. xvi) : ' a mad *Disciple* of hers, Monsieur Porter ' [*sic*]; and *ib.* (p. xix) : ' those who are deluded by the Zealous Pretences of this *Devil* of a *Saint,* to an Extraordinary and Exalted sort of Devotion.'

91. In the Bibliography of her chapter on *William Law and the Mystics* in vol. ix. of *The Cambridge History of English Literature* (1912), Miss C. F. E. Spurgeon says : ' Mlle. Bourignon's works were translated into English' (in 1699, 1703, 1707, 1708, etc.) and much read, more especially in Scotland.' In 1737, it may be added, there appeared a new edition, in English, of her *Renovation of the Gospel Spirit.*

COMMIT THY WAY UNTO THE LORD.

*Commit thy way unto the Lord, and put thy Trust in Him,
and He will bring it to pass.*   Psalm xxxvii, v. 5.

I.

COMMIT *thy way unto the Lord*—Resign
    Thy Self intirely to the Will divine:
All real Good, all Remedy for Ill,
Lies in conforming to His blessèd Will.
By all advice that holy Books afford,
Thou must *Commit thy way unto the Lord.*

II.

And put thy trust in Him.   All other trust,
Plac'd out of Him, is foolish and unjust:
His Loving kindness is the only ground
Where solid Peace and comfort can be found.
What other Prospects either sink or swim,
Do thou stand firm, *And put thy trust in Him.*

III.

And He will bring thy way to pass—The whole
Of all that thou canst wish for to thy Soul
He wills to give it, and thy sinking mind,
By Faith and Patience, cannot fail to find.
To HIM, whatever good Desire it has,
Commit, and Trust, and He will bring to Pass.

AN ILL-TRANSLATED PASSAGE.

St. John's Gospel, chap. II, v. 4: 'Woman what have I to do with Thee?'

A Dialogue.

[Byrom, in the following lines, impugns at length the wording of a passage which naturally enough has incurred much similar comment; and no reader will fail to recognise in his criticism, free as it is one sense, the reverent and loving spirit which was always characteristic of him. It may be noted at once,' that 'woman,' as a form of address, has a very different sound to English ears than 'γύναι' had to Greek. 'Lady' or 'Ma'am' (as addressed to a superior, a parent, or even a sovereign) would be much nearer the mark. Thus 'βασίλεια γύναι' (Eurip. *Electra*, v. 988) should be translated 'royal lady'; and when Talthybius (Eurip. *Hecuba*, v. 508) replies, in the name of the two Atridae and the Achaean host, to her who was once the queen of Ilium as 'γύναι', the word has clearly the same deferential colouring.

Apart from this detail, Byrom's argument against the propriety, and therefore the correctness, of the English rendering of the sentence in the New Testament cited at the beginning of these lines (a reading in which the Revised Version agrees with the Authorised) is carried further than can be held admissible. He points out himself (v. 77) that the Hebrew idiom reproduced in the sentence and fairly translated by the Greek τί ἐμοὶ καὶ σοί may, as his own comparison of parallel passages proves, equally well mean 'What have I to do with thee' or 'What hast thou to do with Me?' and might therefore be rightly, if colloquially, translated, as I find it to be in *The Twentieth Century New Testament* (8th edn., 1901), 'What dost thou want with me?'

If this is so, there can be no harm in admitting that the

translation of the sentence as we have it, if not 'sour and surly,' may at least be described as *primâ facie* rough, and therefore, if its immediate effort be regarded, misleading. But the suggested substitution of 'What would'st thou have Me do?' would, nevertheless, be a mistranslation.

This interesting piece, which, like the next ensuing and some other of the poems in this volume, numbers exactly one-hundred lines, was clearly intended as a dialogue. The letters [B.] (for Byrom) and [C.] have accordingly been prefixed to the lines supposed to be severally spoken by the two inter-locutors.]

[B.] THUS, English version, in some hapless hour,
      Disgrac'd by Phrase so surly and so sour,
Has made one Saviour, without reason why,
To give the Virgin an unkind reply;
For neither text nor context can agree
With 'Woman, what have I to do with thee?'

There was a Marriage, previous words record,
In Cana, where the Mother of our Lord
Then liv'd. As He, and His Disciples too
Were call'd, the numbers which His presence drew   10
Might be the reason why the Wine was done
(No grand provision), when she told her Son
They had no Wine.—Now, that this harmless word
Should cause so harsh an answer, is absurd;
Has not the least connection or design
That can at all relate to want of Wine.

From the supply miraculously wrought
By Jesus afterwards, it has been thought
That she then hinted at relief for Want
Which His Divine ability could grant.   20

10. *Call'd*, invited to the feast.   *of St. John*, chap. ii, v. 2.
' Both Jesus was called, and his   12. (*No grand provision* having
disciples, to the marriage.' *Gosp.*   been made).

Suppose she did—suppose it a Request—
Could such a Hint more meekly be exprest,
Or such an Answer as these words infer
Less meekly, coming from her Son to her?
Unsuitable to ev'ry Phrase, moreo'er,
That follows after, or that goes before.
The very next, 'Mine hour is not yet come,'
If not entire Encouragement, was some
For her to hope that, in due time, the Wine
Would be produc'd by a Command Divine.   30
She took the words directly in this way,
And bade the Servants do what He should say;
Who, in Obedience both to her and Him,
Fill'd up the Urns with water to the brim.

The forc'd construction on Reply so rough,
In all the Comments, makes it plain enough
How Inattention was reduc'd to frame
Its wild conceits about the Virgin's Name.
The Mother's rashness and the Son's rebuke,
Gross and uncouth to first, immediate look,   40
Have no foundation but in mere mistake
Which rash and hasty Commentators make.

[C.] Well, as you paint it, a Contempt so shown
     Ill suits the sacred characters, I own,
     Of Son and Mother. Now, I should be glad
     To hear what sense the passage must have had.
       What would you think it must have been, had She
     Said 'Jesus! What have I to do with Thee!
     They have no Wine; and therefore, fully sure
     That Thou could'st give, I hasten'd to procure.'   50

[B.] Nonsense! You make her hasten to her Son,
     And yet have nothing with Him to be done.

25. It is, moreover, unsuitable.   47-8. Had she, in answer to
                                          the implied reproof, said.

Why, is it not related of the Man
Who was possesst, that, seeing Christ, he ran
To meet Him, tho' far off at the Sea-side,
And ' What have I to do with Thee ? ' he cried ;
' Jesus, Thou Son of God ? ' and then adjur'd
Our Lord to cease the Torment he endur'd ?
Something ' to do with Him,' you see, 'twas true ;
And yet the phrase is : ' What have I to do ? '   60

[C.] It is so, I remember, and confess
The meaning there too difficult to guess.
' What would'st Thou have me do ? ' one thinks, had been
More suited to the case that she was in.

[B.] Right !   You have guessed it ; this is what is meant ;
And the same phrase express'd the mild intent
When Jesus us'd it, to exert His Power,
As Mary will'd Him, in a coming hour.
' What would'st thou have Me do or say ? ' instead
Of incoherent reading, should be read.   70
' Mine hour is not yet come' ; for, when it was,
You see, she thought the thing would come to pass.

[C.] Much plainer this ; will any other place,
Where the same phrase occurs, confirms the Case ?

[B.] Yea ; several.   But I remember none
Where like translation has been fixt upon.
It is an Hebraism, and once, I see,

53. [The man with an unclean spirit] ' cried with a loud voice, and said, What have I to do with thee, Jesus, thou Son of the most high God ? I adjure thee by God, that thou torment me not.' (*St. Mark's Gospel*, ch. v, v. 7.)

59. The unclean spirit, certainly, had something to do with the Saviour, who was about to cast him out.

73. *Place*, passage. (' In sundry places.')

Is render'd : 'What hast thou to do with me ?'
Which Jephthah sends, upon attack begun,
To know what Ammon wanted to have done.   80
'Ye sons of Zeruiah, what have I
To do with you ?' is David's quick reply,
When Abishai, his Captain, would have slain
The Son of Gera; where the sense is plain :
'What would ye have me do?   To go and give
Such Killing orders now?   No—let him live.'
One instance more occurs upon this head :
Sarepta's Widow, when her Son was dead
Said to Elijah : 'What have I to do
With thee, O Man of God ?'   Mind, yet he knew   90
That she had much to do with him, as Grief
Had brought her to him, to obtain relief.
'What shall I do, or say, to Thee' will best
Explain her phrase to the Prophetic guest.

79. See *Judges,* ch. xi, v. 12 : 'And Jephthah sent messages unto the King of the children of Ammon, saying, What hast thou to do with me, that thou art come against me to fight in my land ? '

81. See 2 *Samuel,* ch. xvi, vv. 5, 9, 10 : 'And when King David came to Bahurim, behold, there came out a man of the family of the house of Saul, whose name was Shimei, the son of Gera : he came forth, and cursed still as he came . . . . . . Then said Abishai, the son of Zeruiah, unto the King, Why should this dead dog curse my lord the King? let me go over, I pray thee, and take off his head.   And the King said, What have I to do with you, ye son of Zeruiah ? so let him curse, because the Lord hath said unto him, curse David . . .' The phrase recurs in the same book of *Samuel,* ch. xix, v. 22.

88. See 1 *Kings,* ch. xvii, vv. 17—18 : 'And it came to pass after these things, that the son of the woman, the mistress of the house, fell sick . . . . And she said unto Elijah, What have I to do with thee, O thou man of God ? art thou come unto me to call my sin to remembrance, and to slay my son ? ' Sarepta (Zarephath) is described as a city of Sidon in *St. Luke,* ch. iv, v. 26.

[C.] You've said enough.   No matter, if a phrase
  With other mix'd should other Meaning raise !
  To think that Christ would check by it, or slight,
  The Blessed Virgin never can be right.
  Whatever Mary, full of Grace, might crave,
  As full the gracious Answer that He gave.   100

96. *With other*, with others.   100. *As full* was.

ON THE FALL OF MAN.

PART II.

[In the MS. transcript, these stanzas are superscribed '*Of Man's Obedience, while in Eden blest,*' *Part ii*; the line quoted being the opening line (suggested, of course, by the opening line of *Paradise Lost*) of the stanzas *On the Fall of Man* printed *ante*, vol. ii, pp. 520–3.   This *Second Part* develops more fully the subject of which, in the earlier poem only a part or corner was treated, viz., the supposed anomalousness, or moral absurdity of the current conception of the meaning of the Fall, there denounced as '*a Babel Fiction.*' In the present stanzas, which are in dialogue form (the earlier contained only a small element of dialogue) and which I have printed accordingly, the attempt is made to set out more completely the positive teaching of Law on the subject. It may therefore be well, though Byrom has treated the theme in other poems (see *An Epistle to a Gentleman of the Temple* (in reply to Sherlock), *ante*, vol. ii, pp. 138–166, and the stanzas *On the True Meaning of the Scripture Terms 'Life' and 'Death' when applied to Men*, *ib.*, pp. 376–7, with the *introductory notes* to those pieces) to quote here a longer passage from *An Appeal to all that Doubt or Disbelieve the Truth of the Gospel*, in which Law expounds his view with much lucidity and incisiveness.   The passage will be found pp. 38–9 of the third edn. of *An Appeal* (1768) :

This, and This alone, is the true Nature and Degree of the Fall of Man; it was neither more nor less than this. It was a Falling out of *one World* or Kingdom into *another*, it was changing the Life, Light and Spirit of God, for the Light and Spirit of this World. Thus it was that *Adam* died the very Day of his Transgression, he died to all the Influences and Operations of the Kingdom of God upon him, as we die to the Influences of this World when the Soul leaves the Body; and on the other hand, all the Influences, Operations, and Powers of the Elements of this Life became opened in him, as they are in every Animal at its Birth into this World.

All other Accounts of that Fall, which *only* suppose the Loss of some Moral Perfection, or Natural Acuteness of his Rational Powers, are not only senseless Fictions, but are an express Denial of the Old and New Testament Account of it; for the Old Testament expressly says, that *Adam* was *to die* the *Day* of his Transgression, and therefore it is certain, that He then did die, and that the Fall was his losing his first Life : And to say that he did not die to that first Life in which he was created, is the same Denial of Scripture, as to say, that he did not eat of the forbidden Tree.

Again, the same Scripture assures us, that after the *Fall* his *Eyes were opened;* I suppose this is a Proof, that before the *Fall* they were *shut.* And what is this but saying in the plainest manner, that before the Fall the *Life, Light* and *Spirit* of this World, were *shut* out of him, and that the Opening of his Eyes was only another way of saying, that the Life and Light of this World were opened in him? '].

I.

[A.] You give Occasion, Sir, to ponder more,
    Upon this Point, than one has done before;
    Indiff'rent Action, and a Killing Threat,
    Does seem, indeed, tyrannical; but yet,
    Were not our Parents punish'd at the Time,
    And was not Breach of a Command their Crime?

3. ' But of the tree of the knowledge of good and evil, thou shalt not eat of it : for in the day that thou eatest thereof, thou shalt surely die.' (*Genesis*, ch. ii, v. 17.)

II.

[B.] Breach of Command and Eating was the same,
    On which the Punishment directly came;
    They were inseparable, all the Three,
    And one without the other could not be;   10
    The hurtful Action was the cause of all,
    And God forbade it, to prevent their Fall.

III.

[A.] This puts, I own, if scripturally true,
    Divine Proceeding in a lovelier View;
    But, if the meaning which the words imply
    'Thou shalt not eat,' and 'thou shalt surely die,'
    Be Test and Threat, then positively made,
    You'll contradict the Bible, I'm afraid.

IV.

[B.] The Bible mentions neither Test nor Threat.
    'Thou shalt not eat' was a fair warning, set   20
    Against a foul Temptation to a Guilt;
    And ' thou shalt die,' more plainly, is ' thou wilt ';
    Not God's commanding or forbidding Breath,
    But sinful choice of Ill, brought on the Death.

V.

[A.] "Death"? Let me ask you, do you mean to say
    That Adam died, and Eve, the very Day
    Of Eating—as, in GENESIS, the strict
    And literal construction must predict?
    Did they not both a certain Time survive,
    And he exist some hundred years alive?   30

30. ' And all the days that and thirty years.' (*Genesis*, ch.
Adam lived were nine hundred   v, v. 5.)

VI.

[B.] 'Alive'? To what? Tho' Adam and his Wife
Existed, bare Existence is not Life;
Nor Death [the] loss of Being, but of Bliss:
Devils themselves exist in their abyss.
Now, when his Life of Paradise was fled
That Adam liv'd in, surely he was 'dead.'

VII.

[A.] Why, but no Commentators that I know
Appear to think that he was really so,
But still alive, tho' in a sinfull State.

[B.]   That's the same Thing, unless you love Debate.   40
Reflect, how absolutely near akin
The Scripture page [itself] makes Death and Sin."

VIII.

[A.] It does so, you would mean, and Death I find
To Life superior of this earthly kind.'

[A.] Yes, to be sure. Could God's Monition mean
Dying to this unparadisic Scene,
Which but appear'd, when he presum'd to eat,
And showed the Life according to the meat?

42. *Transcript*: a Death.

42. See, above all, *Romans*, chapters v and vi; and cf. Law, N.S., p. 45: 'And herein plainly appears the true sense of the saying, *God made not Death*, that is, he made not *that* which is *mortal,* or *dying* in the Human Nature, but Sin alone formed and produced that in Man, which could and must die like the Bodies of Beasts.'

47. '. . And he did eat. And the eyes of them both were opened.' (*Genesis,* ch. iii, vv. 6-7.) 'He only saw,' writes Law, *u.s.,* p. 41, ' that he was fallen from his Paradisical glory ' into the condition of the beasts and animals of this world—the ' unparadisic ' state.

48. According to the food which he had eaten.

G

VERSES TO A FRIEND AT HALIFAX,

OCCASIONED BY A LETTER IN THE UNION JOURNAL OF APRIL 13TH, 1759.

[Unfortunately, neither the letter in *The Union Journal* 10 which the superscription of these *Verses* refers nor any copy of that journal itself is discoverable, though enquiries have been instituted both in Manchester and at the British Museum. The identity of the 'friend at Halifax,' to whom another friend had denounced the 'pretended Friend' of the Church, is unknown; of course John Brearcliffe of Halifax, the husband of Byrom's sister Sarah, is out of the question, as he died so early as 1730. It should be remembered that the *Remains* contain but few letters by Byrom dating from these later years of his life.

Readers of this set of verses, prolix like much that Byrom wrote at this time, will not overlook the fact that the protest (for it is virtually such) conveyed by them against the tendency towards denying or ignoring the value of forms in religious worship—gentle as this protest was—clashed with the spirit of the age. Notwithstanding the revival, in some quarters, of a desire for a larger observance of forms, to which attention was incidentally directed above (see the lines *To Mrs. Phebe Byrom ante*, p. 6), a very widespread conviction continued to prevail that 'anything like the worship of God in the beauty of holiness, all that is conveyed in the term symbolism, the due observance of fast and festival—in fact, all those things which to a certain class of minds are almost essential to raise devotion—was still too closely associated with Rome to be capable of being turned to good effect.' (Abbey and Overton, *The English Church in the Eighteenth Century* (new edn., 1887), pp. 307–8).

Byrom's warning is directed against making too much of the objections to the use of eternal accompaniments in the conduct of religious worship. There can be little doubt as to the timely wisdom of his protest, or as to that of his recommendation to accept, without hesitation, what has been established by custom, if reverent in intention and harmless in its actual presentment. But his argument in favour of this sound position is conducted with more diffuseness and looseness than is usual with him; and, although the piece reaches its predestined length of one-hundred lines, it is wanting in finish. The substance of the argument itself is to be found at the close of the Preface *Of Ceremonies, why some be abolished and some retained*, which appeared in the first English *Book of Common Prayer*, of 1549, and was probably written by Archbishop Cranmer. It is still holds its place in the Prayer-book. As to the English practices of bowing at the name of Jesus (directed by the 10th Canon of 1604), of bowing towards the altar on entering and leaving church (recommended by the 7th Canon of 1640), of bowing at the mention of the Incarnation in the Nicene Creed, of turning towards the East in reciting the *Gloria Patri* (said not to be a Roman usage, but to have been enjoined, at different times, by Archbishop Laud and other authorities) and the Creeds, and for references on the subject, see Vernon Staley, *The Ceremonial of the English Church* (2nd edn., Oxford, 1900), pp. 193–9.]

'HARD upon bowing tow'rds the East, indeed,
    And at the name of Jesus in the Creed!'
Well may your Friend at Halifax appeal
To good plain sense from such untoward zeal,
That, with a show of Learning, can produce
Such a burlesque, in fact, upon its use!

As this excessive eagerness to blame
Is that of one who has conceal'd his name.
None can be injur'd, if another show
That this pretended Friend acts like a Foe,   10
And, member of the Church or not, has made
A strange, absurd, pedantical parade,

That comes to nothing but an huge alarm
Against an Usage void of any Harm;
In which, however, he may raise a bawl—
'Evil to him that evil thinks' is all.
Since customs practis'd with a good intent,
That fix no penalty upon dissent,
Amongst the peaceful want no other tie,
Custom itself is Reason to comply.　　　　　　20
Whoever blames it, may enjoy his whim;
But to forbid does not belong to him.

You see, he puts his Readings in array,
Purely to Answer what himself shall say:
Authorities—the best he knew at least—
Are quoted here for turning to the East:
'Arabic Manuscript of Bishop King
And ancient Form have justified the thing;
Arabic Manuscript at Oxford, too,
And Damascen prove its Tradition true;'　　　30
So that, if People should conceive a doubt,
And want old Arabic to help them out,
They have it here for nothing, if they will,
But admiration of the wondrous skill
That could recite what somebody had said
In Manuscriptal Arabic was read,
And furnish an authoritative Store
That Halifax had never known before.
Only to add, that Store of such a sort

16. '*Honni soit qui mal y pense!*'

18. *Upon dissent, i.e.,* from them; customs that are not obligatory.

27. *Bishop King*. This can hardly be *Arch*bishop King; yet I do not know to what other prelate of the name the writer in *The Union Journal* can have referred.

30. *Damascen*. Nicolaus Damascenus, b. 64 B.C., a voluminous Greek historian.

38. *Only to add*. It only remains to add.

Could give the present practice no support;　　40
Much less, undoubtedly, will the antique
Support the wildness of a modern *pique*,
That would excite a clamour thereupon,
Because old Time gave Reasons more than one
For the same thing; since, if it has no ill,
That one's enough to vindicate it still.
"As weak his talk, and sentiment as narrow
As Aristotle, Porphyry and Varro—"
Names, which imply, of course, the namer's learning;
Why else brought in, surpasses all discerning!　　50
But Mother-wit may smile at his whole rental
Of authors Latin, Greek and Oriental,
And harmless Custom, still observ'd, pronounce
His Pound of Clergy lighter than her Ounce.
Heathens, as he has made it out, sometimes
Preferr'd the Eastern to the other Climes:
"That was the place their prayers were pointed at—"
As if the East was any worse for that!
Suppose that Kneeling was a Pagan mode,
Is it what Christians therefore must explode?　　60
What posture, or what gesture, at this rate,
May not be made the subject of debate,
When erudition lumber once has fraught
A mind divested of more native thought!

47-8, 57. Inverted commas *conj.*

46. *That one's,* that one reason is. (But the passage, or the argument, is not very clear.)

48. *Porphyry* (Porphyrius = Purpuratus), the famous Neoplatonist (233—304), whose real name was Malchus (Melek).

Ib. Varro, M. Terentius Varro, 'vir Romanorum eruditissimus.' (*Quintilian*).

51. *Rentall;* roll.

54. *Her, i.e.,* Custom's.

55. Whether or not (though it can hardly be doubted) the custom of worshipping towards the East had its origin in sun-worship, there is great force in the argument of Jeremy Taylor, that the position of the altar governed the direction of the worship. See his tractate *On the Reverence due to the Altar,* cited by V. Staley, *u.s.*

63. *Fraught;* laden.

"Jews," he observes, "in Worship turn'd their face
Wherever dwelling, tow'rds the Holy Place;
Which custom or appointment deem'd design'd
To keep them from Idolatry."   Now, mind,
Turning and bowing at the Sacred Name
Of Jesus may as well design the same   70
As an acknowledgment that Him alone
Who dwelt in Jesus for our God we own;
That, in a Christian sense, we all agree
To us there is no other God but He.
If this be *at* the Heart or *in* the Heart,
When Christians practise an external part,
His criticising upon *"in"* or *"at*
The Name of Jesus" is exceeding flat;
And, let Translation read it "at" or " in,"
Jesus, the Saviour of the World from Sin,   80

65. The ready learning of Mr. I. Abrahams, author of *Jewish Life in the Middle Ages* (1896), who answered an enquiry from me almost by return while away from home, enables me to furnish the following interesting note : In *Daniel* vi, 10, we are told that ' his windows were open in his chamber towards Jerusalem ' when he prayed. Cf. I *Kings,* viii, 48. Now, in Palestine, the synagogues lay east and west (imitating the structure of the Temple where the main entrance was in the east); that this was the case is shown by the ruins of the Galilean synagogues belonging to the Roman period. Hence, in Palestine the worshippers did *not* face the Temple of Jerusalem. But *outside* Palestine, especially in Babylonia, which lay almost due east of Jerusalem, the synagogues were built so that the worshippers turned to Jerusalem in praying (the Talmud attests this in tractate Berahoth 30 a). In Europe, it became customary in the Middle Ages to have the entrances west; so that the worshippers (who pray with backs to the entrance and with faces towards the Ark containing the scrolls, which is in the east) face the east in prayer.   While this remains the general rule, there are numerous exceptions, and the architect is often allowed full licence to choose whatever position best suits the site.   It remains the custom for orthodox Jews, praying *at home,* to face the east during prayer.   This is a well-observed rule still.   In many Jewish houses the eastern wall is marked by a symbol.

76. *Practice an external part,* observe an outward form.

Is still the Same, and neither less nor more
Right-hearted People's Reason to adore,
Or to express their willingness to join
In Adoration by an outward sign.
"Chief Councils," nam'd as if he would discuss,
"Of Nice, Constantinople, Ephesus,
And Chalcedon—in any of the four—"
(And that, suppose that they were all read o'er)
He only tells you, he could [n]ever find
Authority or trace of bowing kind;   90
Then, skips to Queen Elizabeth; and here
Learning concludes the pomp of its career,
Fairly summ'd up in one plain, obvious note—
How short of Reason all the length of Rote!
Here, then, Adieu! Compliance with Desire,
Too far extended, is too apt to tire;
But, if you think that anything remains
Worth reading's patience, or remarking's pains,
If what is left untouch'd shall need a rhyme,
It may be soon bestow'd, another time.   100

81. And reason of right-hearted people for adoring is neither less nor more.

86. Council of Nicæa, 325; of Constantinople, 337 and 381; of Ephesus, 431; of Chalcedon, 451.

94. *Rote*, routine, mere custom.

100. See the following piece.

ON THE ACCEPTANCE AND REJECTION OF FORMS.

[Here we have the ideas which lay at the root of the preceding piece, reproduced in the language of a sincere believer and a follower of the mystical school of thought, and in verse for the most part worthy of the subject, though not quite as limpid as is usual with Byrom.]

I.

A LL is in Man—Good, Evil, Grace, or Sin,
   Heav'n, Earth or Hell, are all of them within,
But—as Experience leaves no room to doubt—
Are manifested by effects without.
Deep underground the Fountain lies conceal'd,
Yet by the Streams that flow from it reveal'd.

II.

They who suppose that any outward scenes
Make up Religion know not what it means;
But outward forms and ceremonies may,
When rightly used, an evidence display   10
Of inward sense that is alike exempt
From too great fondness or too great contempt.

III.

'Tis too great fondness, certainly, to make
Of diff'rent forms, however men mistake,
Matter of mutual censure and debate,
And zeal, too often rising up to hate;
It is no proof of men's Religious claims
To give their neighbours irreligious names.

12. Too great a love of forms, 14. *i.e.*, in their interpretation
or too much disregard for them. or use of them.
13. Too great folly.

IV.

Too great contempt, for any man to call
External Order of no use at all.   20
If he were really so compleat a Saint
That, for his own account, he did not want,
He would the more unwillingly forbid
Its well-meant use to any one that did.

V.

Partiality, indeed, in diff'rent sects
Creates a world of mischievous effects;
Bigots for one, had any else been theirs,
Would have been bigots for the form it wears.
In all the hot, the bitter and the sour,
Forms of Religion are without the pow'r.   30

VI.

But they who practise with an honest view,
Such as their birth or breeding led them to,
Behaving mildly, where their lot shall fall,
Thinking no ill and wishing well to all—
The heart-discerning Blesser of the meek
Will hear their Pray'r, and give them what they seek.

VII.

Some men, perceiving faults in ev'ryone,
Reject all forms, and will comply with none.
Of these, the careless their objections plead,

19. It is too great contempt.
22. Had no need for its use.
27. Bigots in upholding one sect, had they belonged to another, would have been equally bigots in upholding its particular form. Cf. ' By the simple accident of birth, *You* might have been High Priest to Mumbo-Jumbo.' (Hood's *Ode to Rae Wilson*.)
30. *Without the pow'r, i.e.,* of religion.
35. God, Who knows the heart and blesses the meek in spirit.

And live at large, as present fancies lead;   40
The stricter few, by other thoughts impell'd,
Think all so wrong that none should be upheld.

VIII.

These rarer Souls I leave for what they be,
For Judgment of them is too high for me:
This or that man—let greater skill decide
If led by Piety, or led by Pride;
If, whilst abroad professing not to roam,
He has a Christ, or Anti-Christ, at Home.

47. Whether, while professing not to stray from the right path.

INTOLERANCE OF FORM.

[This long and not particularly striking piece has little in
it that is distinctly Byromic, unless it be the very first
couplet.   The subject recalls that of *Verses to a Friend at
Halifax,* whether or not these lines were provoked by the same
publication, evidently (see vv. 19–22) the work of a writer
who had attracted attention both by his prose and by his
verse.   But the treatment here is even less incisive.]

' KNOW him?' Not I; let him be who he will,
    I wish him well, but think he reasons ill;
And, when the Lines which you thought fit to print
Had plainly fix'd his argumental Stint,
That he should chose to be so meanly witty,
Beside the Matter, is—the more the Pity!

4. 'Stint' is measure or proportion.   The interpunctuation
of these and the next two lines
in the MS. rather confuses their
meaning; but, as interpunctuated
above, they seem to give sense.

'Beside the matter' is 'away
from the point.'   It would be
possible to interpunctuate:
        ' so meanly witty!
    Besides, the Matter is——'
But this seems forced.

But, passing by, as neither fair not fit,
Tho' easy to return, such kind of wit—
The certain Sign, when coming from the Press,
Of argument reduc'd to sore Distress—   10
For sake of many who, his Letters said,
Wanted to clear their doubts upon this head,
And, consequently, mind, in search of Light,
Not who the writers are, but what they write:
The properest Revenge is to disperse
One cloudy Streak, amidst the shining Verse,
That moves along, with *'Papist'* at its Tail,
In Shape of Reason, tho' the Substance fail;
And, by his gracious Rhime—since all men know
That he has got two Strings unto his Bow,   20
Both Prose and Verse, and the prosaic String,
Ere Heart had scorch'd it, gave the daring fling—
Let it appear, with all the Strength it had,
When first he show'd the Custom to be bad!
'Bowing,' he says, 'is wrong, and tow'rds the East
Is Pagan, Jewish, Popish at the least,'
From all assemblies Protestant it ought
To be expell'd by his decisive Thought.
Should they ask, 'Why? What Evil has it done,
That such aversion should be now begun   30
To custom kept, as his own proofs evince,
Before the name of Protestant, and since;
And, when Reformers from the Church of Rome
(As wise as he, they may as yet presume,
Till his superior Wisdom shall appear ,
And make anonymous Decision clear)
Saw nothing in this Custom to reform—
Why now against it such a sudden Storm?'

13. *Mind,* give their attention to.

30-1. That a late beginning should now be made of objection to usages observed both before and since the Reformation.

This want to have a point clear'd up can meet
No solid answer in the learnèd sheet.   40
   The specious Turn (for he could hardly miss
Putting the Question to himself) is this:
I fancy, most Conformists never heard
Of any reason for the use aver'd,
Nor can give any, but that 'tis in use.
'This,' he observes, 'is but a weak Excuse;
For, by the same, False-worshipping may run
To universal Practice, once begun;
If, by mankind's corruption, once it get
An Introduction, Custom will abet.'   50
This is the Trophy on each Bowstring hung
Of learnèd Prose, and Verse in Vulgar Tongue—
As poor a Fallacy as ever caught
The Dupes of Hate, in their Neglect of Thought!
Good Customs, or good manners, that obtain
Can want no other answer, it is plain;
Or, if indifferent and nothing bad,
For them there needs no other to be had;
But, if profane and wicked, it is true,
So is th' excuse, and it will never do.   60
The Guilt of this should therefore, first, be shown;
For, whilst the Proof is, like the Man, unknown,
Who shall decide, if Banishment be fit,
Which it belongs to—whether him or it?
   In any Point to Christian choice left free
When Protestants and Papists both agree,
To drone out 'Popery' and 'Superstition'
Is neither Sense, nor Wit, nor Condition.
If Popish Doctrine, Presbyterianism,
Or some cant word that ends in *ish* or *ism*,   70
Be proof that anything be right or wrong,
'Tis Proof alike in all Professions strong,

47. *False-worshipping,* a false   68. *Condition,* good manners.
or heterodox form of worship.

And no Profession can be well profest
But by devoutly hating all the rest.
    He makes a crime of bowing in the Creed.
Suppose the daring Fancy to succeed,
What is the consequence?   A num'rous Tribe
Of other Fancies, endless to describe,
Of Censures, waiting, after one is past,
On Bowing, first, on Creed itself at last.   80
Witness the Letter: 'Men of Sense,' says he,
'And Penetration, certainly must see,
That 'tis a thing improper, and absurd,
To pay more Rev'rence to the Name, or Word,
Of " Son " than " Father "; to distinguish, too,
" Jesus " from " Joshua "—from names enoo':
" Emanuel," " Christ," " Messiah," and the rest
By which the selfsame Person is exprest.'
He did not see, how this preverted strength
Of Reas'ning gulls upon the Text, at length,   90
Where such Distinction to one Name alone
Above, and in, and under Earth is shown—
To that of Jesus; and they all fulfill,
In honouring the Son, the Father's Will.
All Christian men, and women, too, if Sense
Will penetrate thro' ev'ry vain Pretence
That would forbid a reverential Frame
Of Mind, and Body, at the Blessèd Name
Of Jesus, the Almighty Lord, by Whom
Health, and Salvation, to a Soul must come.   100

86. Joshua's own name was Oshea; the name of *Jehoshua* or *Joshua* (Saviour), of which *Jesus* is the Greek reproduction, was given to him by Moses, perhaps because of his having been in command at the great victory over Amalek in Rephidim.

90. *Gulls upon*, stultifies.

91. *Philippians*, ch. ii, vv. 9-10: ' Wherefore God also hath . . . . given him a name which is above every name: That at the name of Jesus every knee shall bow, of things in heaven, and things in earth, and things under the earth.'

GOSPEL TRUTH AND ITS PROOFS.

[This poetical epistle, in many ways characteristic of its author and of the spirit in which he regarded Biblical criticism, touches on more than one theological problem, a satisfactory treatment of which, as Byrom, with his usual modesty, declares, 'surpassed his critical skill.' Yet, in 1756—probably not long before he wrote the present lines—he had discussed the first part of their theme, viz., the Pentecostal Miracle, at considerable length in a communication addressed to the same correspondent (see *ante*, vol. ii, pp. 282–304). This was Peter Lancaster, vicar of Bowdon in Cheshire (as to whom see *introductory note, ib.*, p. 282, where reference is made to his publications on prophetic and apocalyptic subjects).

From the opening lines it appears that Byrom, before writing the letter, had sent for a 'pamphlet of Hare's.' Thomas Hare, Rector of Chedington,[1] Misterton, Somerset, from 1757 to 1762 (the year of his death), is stated in Hutchins' *History of Dorset*, vol. ii, to have been "a good scholar and poet, and" to have "translated the Odes of Horace with no small degree of success." In 1758, he published *A New*

---

1. Cf. l. 60 : ' his Chedington count.' Thanks to this clue, and the information kindly given by the Rev. T. Guy Morres, the present rector of Chedington, I was able to identify his predecessor as the ' Hare ' in question. The reference in the text was suggested to me by Mr. Morres. Mr. J. A. Venn informs me that a Thomas Hare, of Simonsbury, Dorset, is stated in Foster's *Alumni Oxonienses* to have matriculated at Oxford from Trinity College in 1725 and to have proceeded B.A. in 1729 and M.A. in 1744; while no Thomas Hare appears to have graduated from any College at Cambridge between the years 1673 and 1827. On the other hand, a second Thomas Hare matriculated at Oxford in 1783 (aged 26), as son of the Rev. Thomas Hare of Crewkerne—our author.

Explanation of Daniel's 70 weeks, wherein (it is conceived) all difficulties are removed with which all other attempts of this kind have been embarrassed. This is manifestly the pamphlet to which Byrom's letter (dated New Year's day, 1760) makes reference. He was also, as appears from the title-page of that production, Master of the School of Crewkerne in Somersetshire, which is not far from Chedington.

A review of Thomas Hare's *Explanation of Daniel's Prophecy* appeared in vol. xx of *The Monthly Review, or, Literary Journal* (1759), which gives a sufficient account of his explanation. The four verses, *Daniel*, ch. ix, vv. 24–27, which form the communication of Gabriel to the Prophet, are thus translated by Hare :

' *Ver.* 24. Seventy weeks are determined upon thy people and upon thy holy city, to curb or restrain rebellion [or destruction], to fill up the measure of sins, to make reconciliation for iniquity, and to bring in everlasting righteousness, and to confirm the truth of the vision and prophet, and to anoint the most holy.

' 25. Know, therefore, and understand. From the going forth of the commandment to restore and to build Jerusalem unto Messiah the ruler shall be seventy-seven weeks ; threescore and two[weeks] are to be counted back again [that is from Messiah the ruler], and then the street shall be built, and the wall even in troublous times.

'26. And after these threescore and two weeks [the following events shall be seen in due time :] Messiah shall be cut off, but not for himself [or for his own fault], and the people of the governor that shall come shall destroy the city and the sanctuary, and the end thereof shall be with a flood, and to the end of the war desolations are determined.

'27. And he [the governor that shall come] shall establish a treaty of peace with many during one week [or a course of seven years], and in the midst of the week he shall cause the sacrifice and the oblation to cease ; and with wings of abominations he shall spread desolation even to utter destruction, and [the destruction] being determined shall be poured out on the desolate.

The 'commandment' in v. 25, Hare supposes to be the decree for rebuilding and restoration of Jerusalem, issued by Cyrus, the first and principal edict from which the others took their rise. Although only the building of the Temple is mentioned in the account of the decree of Cyrus given by Ezra (ch. i), yet the same King Cyrus did really order the building of the city, as well as of the Temple, of Jerusalem; for, when he gave the Jews liberty to return to their own country, he must certainly have allowed them to build houses for their habitation there; and that they actually did begin to build the city by reason of Cyrus' decree, though they were hindered from making any great progress in the work, appears from Ezra, ch. iv, vv. 12 sqq., and Haggai, ch. i, v. 4.

The decree of Cyrus, usually dated 536 B.C., which Hare treats as the starting-point of the prophetical calculation, he takes as having been issued in the year of the Julian period 4183, or rather (by omitting the actual year of issue) from the Passover of 4184. From this time he reckons on to the thirteenth year of our Lord's age, the Julian year 4723, when He first exerted His pre-eminence in the Temple, and thus first showed Himself as 'Messiah the ruler'—the Hebrew word employed being the ordinary designation of the Master or ruler of the Temple. From 4184 to 4723 are 539 years, or seventy-seven weeks (periods of seven years each). Hereupon, reckoning back from 4723, he reaches the year of the Julian period 4289, which he regards as coinciding with the fortieth year of Artaxerxes I (Longimanus), usually given as 425, 'in which the building and re-establishment of the new city of Jerusalem was finished.'

In computing the seventy weeks 'determined upon' Jerusalem—the *crux* of the problem—Hare, instead of, like most previous commentators, adding the one week of v. 27 to the seven weeks, and threescore and two weeks, of v. 26, so as to make up the required number of seventy, treats the seventy (or all but seventy) weeks and the one week separately. Adding seventy weeks (or 490 years) to the date of 4289, he reaches the 66th year (465) of the Christian era, in which, during the reign of Nero, occurred the revolt of the Jews against the Roman dominion, in consequence of which many thousands of Jews were slain by Gessius Florus, Governor of Judæa, and Cestius Gallus, governor of Syria, invested Jerusalem. The Jewish war thus begun was brought to an overwhelming close under Vespasian seven years later, and this makes up the one 'week' to which the last verse of the prophecy (v. 27) refers.

It is not my 'province' to attempt in this place an enquiry into the soundness of Hare's explanation. While the statements of Josephus (*Bellum Judaicum*, from bk. ii, c. 14 onwards; cf. Merivale, *History of the Romans under the Empire*, ch. lix) sufficiently bear out his reference to the Neronian revolt and its results (the sack of Jerusalem, of course, took place in 70; but the reduction of the country may be held to have extended over a few further years), the *terminus a quo* of his entire computation is open to grave doubts, inasmuch as there is no proof, even if there were any likelihood, of either Cyrus (notwithstanding Hare's specious argument) or Artaxerxes having ordered the rebuilding of the *city* of Jerusalem. Whether the further objection be well grounded that it is impossible to consider the author of the Book of Daniel—or the Divine Author of the revelation itself—as beginning the whole computation from the act of a pagan sovereign, it is not for me to decide; in *Isaiah*, ch. xlv, v. 1, Cyrus is termed 'the Lord's Anointed.'

For a terse but most instructive examination of the whole question see the notes and summary in S. Oettli and J. Meinhold's *Die geschichtlichen Hagiographen und das Buch Daniel*, forming section 8 of part A of H. Strack and O. Zöckler's *Kurzgefasster Kommentar zu den heiligen Schriften Alten und Neuen Testamentes* (Nördlingen, 1889). The view of these commentators is opposed to the traditional Messianic interpretation of the prophecy; they regard this and the previous chapter as later in date of composition than the period of the exile, and the reference in v. 26 as being to the murder of the High Priest Onias IV by Andronicus, Governor under Antiochus IV (187—164 B.C.). (*ii Maccabees*, ch. iv, v. 34.)

Byrom, while abstaining from any criticism of Hare's general argument, except in so far as he suggests its superfluousness, in stanza viii says that Hare reckons as seventy weeks the

H

seven weeks of the Vulgate. Oettli and Meinhold interpunctuate '7 *Siebenheiten*'; and '62 *Siebenheiten*'; but our Authorised Version (and, for that matter, the Vulgate also) adds the threescore and two to the seven, and places a : after the second 'weeks,' so that the total is 69 (70). Since Hare's pamphlet itself is unfortunately inaccessible, his divergence, on which Byrom comments, must be concluded to be the same as that of the modern critics. The rest of his criticism is merely illustrative of the uncertainty as to the correct translation of the Hebrew word to be rendered, in Hare's opinion, 'seventy' or 'seven' according to the pointing.]

I.

D EAR Vicar,   January 1st, 1760.
    The subject inclin'd me to send
For this Pamphlet of Hare's, to present an old Friend
With the sight of a Comment so nice and so new,
And mistakes all remov'd, if the Author say true.
It will come by your neighbour, the Baguley Squire,
Who, when he complied with the Donor's desire,
Said : 'I'll hand it myself to the Bowdon divine,
When I go—and perhaps you'll enclose him a line.'

II.

I guess'd what he meant, and I thought, So I will;
Though the Matter surpasses my critical Skill,   10
I can settle one point in Chronology clear,
Which is—that I wish him a happy New Year.
As to those which the Rector has treated upon,
Having no settled judgment, 'tis best to make none;
But if he who has studied the question give leave
To expect his Decision, I'll wait to receive.

1. One of Peter Lancaster's own publications was *A Chronological Essay on the IXth Chapter of Daniel* (1722).

5. *The Baguley Squire*, John Houghton, whose first wife was the younger sister of Byrom's wife and first cousin Elizabeth (Byrom). Cf. vol. ii, p. 282, *note, ante.*

13. *The Rector* of Chedington. See *introductory note.*

16. *Receive* it.

III.

There are two sorts of Proof, it comes into my Mind,
Of Miraculous one, one Prophetical kind;
Which the learnèd have writ many volumes about,
To deduce how the Gospel is true beyond doubt.   20
But it must be confess'd, that the dissonant schemes,
Which the learnèd embrace upon both the two themes,
Give a handle to Deists, who barely deny,
Tho' without any scheme of their own, to Reply.

IV.

That the Gospel is true, from its Miracles wrought
And its having fulfilled what the Prophets had taught,
Is a fact, in itself, of a nature so plain
That objections, though puzzling, are all of them vain.
But, when certain Divines talk of Miracles ceas'd
(An assurance of which must imply one at least),   30
How, in this or that Age, they existed no more,
I wonder what Gospel has taught such a Lore?

V.

In the Scripture, throughout, is there any one word
That confines them to Ages, first, second or third,
Or to any succeeding? That men should pretend
To debate in what Century they had an end—
On the first if a Middleton fancies to fix,

37. In, *conj.* for MS. *Or.*

21. *Dissonant schemes.* Dissonant, or different, as resting on
the argument from miracles and
on that from prophecy, respectively.

23. *Barely deny,* simply refuse.
30. *One* miracle.

34. *Them, i.e.,* miracles.

37. Dr. Conyers Middleton's *A
Free Inquiry into the miraculous
Powers, which are supposed to
have subsisted in the Christian
Church from the earliest ages,
through several successive cen-
turies,* to which is prefixed *The
Introductory Discourse* (1747),
was followed (in 1748) by *A
Vindication of the Free Inquiry
from the Objections of Dr.
Dodwell and Dr. Church.* Both
are reprinted in vol. i of Middleton's *Miscellaneous works*
(1752). He maintains at length
the statement of his Preface that
' according to my principles,
miraculous powers never subsisted at all, after the days of the
Apostles.'

And opponents advance up to four, five, or six—
Is the proof of the Gospel their principal Scope,
Or the love of Contention, and fear of the Pope?   40

VI.

In Prophetical case, if an Author, who seeks
To interpret the secret of difficult weeks,
Finds a new Explanation, and thinks it exempt
From the faults which embarrass each other attempt—
Were the pure, simple truth of the Gospel concern'd
Whether he, in due form, had corrected the learn'd,
Its proof would appear, in too great a degree,
A more difficult point than one takes it to be.

VII.

'Tis well, when a Critic tries critical pains
Upon matters abstruse, if he really explains;   50
And to true and sound learning the labours belong,
To confute the Sophistic that takes a thing wrong.
But, whoever objects, or whoever confutes,
The Gospel is free from their learnèd disputes;
Its force in the heart the most simple and meek
Are enabl'd to feel, without Hebrew and Greek.

41. *In Prophetical case.* As to the matter of prophecy, or argument from prophecy, if an author finds a new and to him perfectly satisfactory solution of an old difficulty—supposing the question whether he were proved right to affect the cardinal question as to the truth of the Gospel, the proof of this would be made to appear far more difficult than it really is. In other words: the truth of the Gospel depends on something else than the soundness of any particular argument from prophecy.

42. *Difficult weeks.* See *introductory note.*

52. *Sophistic* learning.

VIII.

This learnèd Hebræan proposes, I find,
To adopt a Construction of singular kind.
Sev'n Weeks, as our Vulgate has made the amount,
Are Sev'nty and Sev'n, in his Chedington count,   60
To Messiah the Prince (rather, ' Ruler,' says Hare
Because, without Points, such a reading is fair,)
But, though, by all Proofs, Punctuation in view,
His positions may seem rather artful than true.

IX.

But this be your Province !—I'll only remark
On a text, *en passant,* that appears to be dark
By misrend'ring of שׁבוּע : Seven Sons of a Jew
(Look at *Acts*, the nineteenth) were but, probably, two;
Some versions say ' Sev'n,' and yet, after, say ' Both;'
Now, as שׁבוּע,   you know, may be 'Week,' 'Sev'n,' or   70
    ' Oath,'
Perhaps, the two Sons, using Paul's adjuration,
Have been made to be 'Sev'n' by mistaken Translation.

X.

'Sev'n Sons,' all Exórcists !   All, naked and wounded,
Fled away from one Man ?   This, I doubt, is ill-founded.

57. *Hebræan,* Hebrew scholar.

62. *Without points.* It will be remembered that John Hutchinson, the author of *Moses's Principia* (1724), maintained that Hebrew, when read without points, would confirm his theories. (See *Moses's Principia*, p. 132, *post*.)

68. *Acts,* ch. xix, vv. 13-14 : ' Then certain of the vagabond Jews, exorcists, took upon them to call over them which had evil spirits the name of the Lord Jesus . . . And there were seven sons of one Sceva, a Jew, and chief of the priests . . .' The Authorised and the Revised Version agree as to the number seven.

73. *Ib.,* v. 16 : 'And the man in whom the evil spirit was leaped on them, and overcame them, and prevailed against them, so that they fled out of that house naked and wounded.'

He prevail'd ἐπ' ἀμφοτέρων —'*super ambobus*'—
That reading, at least, can but suit with '*Duobus.*'
But, to draw tow'rds an end : where the Gospel is spread,
It becomes its own proof of what Prophecy said;
One Miracle now, and one Prophecy too,
Is enough to evince it Infallibly true.   80

XI.

Of human existence the marvellous Plan—
Of the birth of a Child growing up to a Man,
Of the wonders relating to Body and Soul,
Tho' a common, not less a miraculous Whole—
So plead[s] for the Truth, without Learning or Art,
That the free to conviction soon have it at heart,
Soon see what the aim is, and always has been,
Of Nature without and of Gospel within.

XII.

And the certain Prediction, which none will deny,
That, man, woman, child, we must all of us die,   90
Though the week, day or moment be hid and unknown,
Is a proof by which all may be Prophets their own ;
May foresee, what the Law and the Prophets evince,
The Return of a glorious Messiah, the Prince,
To Redeem from this World, and to raise up, good Men,
Like so many Daniels, safe out of its Den.

75. The Greek text (*Nw. Test.* ed. C. Tischendorf, Leipzig, 1850) reads : κατακυριεύσας ἀμφοτέρων ἴσχυσεν κατ' αὐτῶν.

76. *Duobus, i.e.,* if ' both ' is held to be the correct translation of שׁנֵי instead of ' seven.'

81. The marvellous plan of human existence—the mystery of birth and growth, and that of the union of body and soul.

THE LIFE IMMORTAL.

[Many passages of Scripture might, of course, be quoted in illustration of these fine stanzas and of their concluding couplet. Perhaps, this one passage will suffice: 'For the law of the Spirit of life in Christ Jesus hath made me free from the law of sin and death . . . . . . For to be carnally minded is death; but to be spiritually minded is life and peace.' *Romans*, ch. viii, vv. 2, 6.]

I.

THERE is, if men will understand the case,
  A life of Nature and a life of Grace—
The first, an eager, anxious, restless life,
Or nature's properties in kindling strife;
A want, a longing, a desire of bliss,
That cannot reach, or find out what it is.

II.

The second is the blessèd Life Divine,
That in the Darkness of the first must shine;
Must raise its own true light in it, to give
The Scripture's deeper meaning of 'to live'—   10
Its own own true Spirit, whose life-giving breath
If wanting, Life is but, in Scripture, Death.

III.

Without both Lives, no Creature could be made,
No more than Light be bounded without Shade;
No Creature wanted, in creating hour,
Its proper beauty, colour, form or pow'r;
Nor, if Intelligent, an able will,
Free from all hindrance, to retain them still—

12-3. In the absence of the life-giving breath of the Spirit of the Divine Life, the life of nature is only what Scripture calls death.

15. In the hour of its creation.

IV.

For ever to retain, and to be true
To them whose Goodness had no ill in view;   20
Who formed and fill'd with its enliv'ning flood
The Creature, capable of endless good.
He that enslaves himself, created free—
Who is the Cause of all his Ills but he?

V.

Not bare existence, when we go from hence,
Is Immortality, in Scripture sense;
For thus alike immortal are confest
The good, the bad, the ruin'd and the blest—
All must exist, where'er they chuse to dwell,
Angels in Heav'n, or self-made Friends in Hell.   30

VI.

God's Light and Spirit, dwelling in the Soul,
Make, as at first, its blest, immortal whole;
'Tis Death to want them; vain is all Dispute:
The Gospel only reaches to the Root.
All the Inspired have understood it thus:
'Immortal Life is that of Christ for Us.'

20. ' Them ' seems to refer to the qualities mentioned in l. 16 above.

26. ' God, Who will render . . . to them who by patient continuance in well-doing seek for glory and honour and immortality, eternal life.' (*Romans*, ch. ii, vv. 5-7.)

27. For this would mean that all are alike immortal.

FORMS OF PRAYER.

'My friends, it is become a matter of some debate amongst you, in what method prayer, and *especially public prayer*, is most properly performed, whether by reading Prayers already composed, confining our thoughts to the sense of what is read; or by free and *extempore* Prayer, dictated by the sense, state and disposition of our *own* minds, and accommodated to any occasion or event of life' etc. *The Scripture Account of Prayer*, by John Taylor, D.D. [1761], pp. 10–11.

[The moderation of the following plea for established forms of prayer will not remain unnoticed, nor the true piety of spirit which pervades it. The question here raised is one on both sides of which there is much to be said, and much that will continue to be said not only in different religious communities, but at different periods in the history of those communities. The history of Presbyterianism, for instance, could not have been what it was, had the practice of 'free and extempore' prayer been from the first either eschewed or restricted in it.

An eager controversy had arisen on the subject to which reference is made in Byrom's quotation from the posthumous work of Dr. John Taylor, a nonconformist divine who during the last three or four years of his life held the office of tutor in divinity and moral philosophy in the newly-founded Warrington Academy (and who of course is not to be confounded with Byrom's friend and shorthand 'brother,' the editor of Lysias), in consequence of the attempt begun in 1750 to introduce 'public forms' into nonconformist worship. A meeting of dissenting ministers to this end was held at Warrington in 1750. By 1760, this attempt had progressed so far that it was resolved to build at Liverpool a chapel for non-conformist liturgical worship, and Taylor and other ministers were invited to prepare a book of prayer. On the other hand, John Seddon, the secretary of the Academy (of which he was afterwards created rector) took up the scheme warmly, and to him was attributed a *Letter to a Dissenting Minister, representing the expediency of stated Forms of Prayer for Public Worship*.　It was against this proposal that Taylor lifted up his voice; but *A Form of Prayer and a New Collection of Hymns*, edited by Seddon with two coadjutors, was actually published in 1763, two years after Taylor's death, and used for some thirteen years in the Octagon Chapel, Liverpool.　(See *Dict. of Nat. Biog.*, vols. li and lv, arts. *Seddon, John*, and *Taylor, John*.)

Manifestly, as Byrom points out himself (ll. 75 *sqq.*), the question at issue here is a wholly different one from that with which he had dealt in *To the Rev. Messrs. H— and H— on Preaching Extempore* (vol. i, pp. 101–5); but it may be worth pointing out, that, as would indeed appear from ll. 91–2 of the present poem, Byrom was an advocate of extempore preaching, and thought that the Church of England could only gain from the general adoption of a practice common to all other Christian Churches.　Habit, however, in this case proved stronger than example, and was quite equal to the task of discovering arguments in its own favour.]

‘FREE and *Extempore*’?　The title ‘free,’
　　Join'd with *Extempore*, will scarce agree,
So as to give extemporaneous care
The preference to Form of Common Prayer;
‘Method’ and ‘Public’ seeming to import
Performance of some regulated sort.
　　Pray'r, it is justly noted, is the Part,
Not of the Tongue or Language, but the *heart*.
Want of an Heart no eloquence supplies
That precompos'd, or sudden, thoughts devise;　　10
And one who is dispos'd aright to pray

5. There seems to be some sort of allusion here to the term *methodists*—persons who regulate their practice by theory—a word employed in reference to medical men long before it was used of those who, in Warburton's phrase, had " in the days of our forefathers, been called ‘ precisians.' "

Will soon be heard, whatever *it* shall say.
It is itself the Form which God requires,
Ready to grant its well-conceiv'd desires;
Tho' with unutter'd earnestness it burn,
He, too, can make th' unspeakable Return.
Suppose an heart in so devout a frame,
Will proper words put out its purer Flame,
Unless just new brought forth upon the spot?
Will reading quench it, and pronouncing not?   20
Will forms, approv'd by Christian ages past,
If pure themselves, extinguish it at last,
And new, *Extempore* invented Phrase,
With its continual variation, raise?
For praying Hearts the wand'ring scheme appears
Not so commodious as for itching ears,
And minds not over-prone to be devout,
With a liturgic service, or without.
Crude, unpremeditated prayer, you see,
Is next excluded from the name of 'free,'   30
And justly, too; tho', still, it has the claim
To its allowed extemporary Fame;
And, therefore, 'free,' whatever it include,
No more defines '*Extempore*' than 'Crude.'
Free prayer, 'tis argued, furnishes the mind
With good material, of a proper kind—
Digested language, order, and so on:
In terms from which, if singly dip'd upon,
Readers would judge that the design'd affair
Was Commendation of liturgic Prayer;   40
So that the two most fundamental Laws,
As here laid down for settling of the cause—
To wit, that Pray'r from eloquence and art

---

12. *It*, i.e., the heart.
25. *The wand'ring scheme.*
The scheme of praying without
adherence to any set form.

38. *If singly dip'd upon.* If
taken singly.
39. *The design'd affair.* The
object in view.

Is not acceptable, but from the *heart*;
And, then, that previous care is to digest,
Connect, and order words to be exprest—
Do, by immediate sequel of their own,
Infer, that words should publicly be known,
If all the flock must, with their hearts, unite
And join the Pastor where he shall recite.   50
    'Tis difficult, indeed, without such aid
To think how Pray'r, as public, shall be made,
Or by the public—for, do people pray
By barely hearing what a man shall say,
Truly or crudely, as he goes along,
With speech untaught beforehand, to the Throng?
Can they be said, or be oblig'd, to make
His language theirs, or, maybe, his mistake?
If so, it is confess'd that, crude or free,
They pray *Extempore* as much as he—   60
More so, perhaps; for he, by private law,
May come prepar'd with what they never saw,
And, use of forms forbidding, he alone,
'Tis possible, may use one of his own,
Which, if well worded, may encrease the storm
In favour of a *Gift* against a Form—
The ' Gift of Prayer,' here mentioned and defin'd
To be attainment of imperfect kind,
Without the spirit, or a praying Frame
Of Heart. But how can any 'gifted' claim   70
Subsist without it, when a juster Phrase
Had said before : ' It is the heart that prays?'
How, then, can this be call'd the '*Gift of Pray'r*'
In which the heart and spirit has no share?
By its own rules, it seems as if the book
Preaching for praying frequently mistook;
For sev'ral maxims in it have occur'd,

61. In accordance with a law   74. *i.e.*, Taylor's.
which he has made for himself.

In point of Preaching, true; of Pray'r, absurd—
Just as absurd as if the Clark alone
Should sing a stave of Psalmody, his own,   80
Without a form, and, list'ning to the thing,
The Congregation should be said to sing.
    Easy mistake—for, where there is no use
Of Forms, the Ministers alone produce
Free Pray'r, as it is call'd; and thus they teach
The people words, and may be said to 'preach'
As well as pray; and tho' they may divide
These two, [their] Praying makes them coincide;
And hence, against all ancient fact, some hold
That Christians had no Liturgies of old.   90
So Methodists, they fancy, by free pray'r
Draw from the Church such numbers to their chair.
Fact is, extemporary Preaching gains
The crowded audience by its own free strains—
Not from the Church, where yet at least they pray
By stated Forms in her established way.
Between two ways tho' men are free to halt,
A Form, as such, in short, is not in fault;
Nor will new Prayr's come soon, from any class,
Better than what the Church already has.   100

88. *Transcript* : then.

90. The question here summarily decided cannot be dismissed in a brief note. Public worship in general (λειτουργία, *missa*) seems to have been first divided into parts and formalised in the period reaching from Constantine the Great to the Council of Chalcedon (324—451); the Roman liturgy connected with the Lord's Supper received its present form from Gregory the Great (d. 604). Cf. Gieseler, *Compendium of Church History*, Engl. tr. by Davidson, vol. ii, pp. 46, 145. Taylor, p. 53, roundly asserts that St. Chrysostom's declaration, ' God recketh not the eloquence of the tongue, nor the elegant composition of words,' furnishes 'another Proof, that set forms of Prayer were not in use in St. Augustine's time, full four hundred years after Christ.'

METHODISTS AND THEIR PREACHERS.

[This and the two following pieces are alike concerned with
Methodism, and there can hardly be a doubt that the present
piece and its immediate successor refer to the same event,
the preaching 'in the Square,' by a preacher whom the second
piece identifies as Whitefield. 'The Square' can be no other
than St. Ann's Square, identified in the present piece by the
mention of the Church, if not by the apparent allusion to
'Mountebank Green.' But there are difficulties in the way of
fixing the date of the event—difficulties which could be
removed at once, had it proved possible to procure a copy of
the number or numbers of *Whitworth's Magazine*, which are
discussed in the second and third pieces.

According to Axon's *Annals of Manchester*, p. 82, John
Wesley visited Manchester from March 16th to 19th, 1738, and
then preached at Salford Chapel (of which immediately) and
at St. Ann's. But he can hardly, on that occasion, have
preached in 'the Square'; for he is stated not to have followed
Whitefield's example of open-air preaching till April 2nd,
1739, when he addressed about three thousand people in an
open ground adjoining the city of Bristol. Although he
frequently visited Manchester afterwards, I can find no
mention of his having preached there in the open air, in
St. Ann's Square or elsewhere.

Whitefield's first visit to Manchester seems to have been
that of December, 1738, of which he makes mention in his
Diary (Part ii), cited in *Remains*, vol. ii, p. 218, where he
states that he reached Manchester on Saturday, the 2d of the
month, and on the following Sunday preached twice at Mr.
Clayton's chapel (Holy Trinity Chapel, Salford), having
indeed come 'so far out of his way,' for the benefit of 'dear
Mr. Clayton's judicious Christian conversation.' John
Clayton, who had also been the magnet that had attracted
Wesley to Manchester in the previous April, was a

Manchester man by birth and breeding, and had been a prominent member of the Oxford circle from which sprang the Methodist Society. A full account of him will be found in Canon Raines' *Fellows of the Collegiate Church of Manchester*, edited by Dr. Renaud for the Chetham Society, part ii, 1891; see, also, Mr. C. W. Sutton's notice of him in *Dict. of Nat. Biog.*, vol. xi. He was a staunch Jacobite and a zealous High Churchman, and a great friend of Byrom. According to Tyerman (*Life of Whitefield*, vol. i, p. 148), besides preaching twice in Mr. Clayton's church 'to thronged and attentive congregations,' he 'assisted six more clergymen in administering the Sacrament to 300 communicants.' He had been ordained deacon at Oxford in 1736, and hence is called (l. 28) 'a brother clergyman,' and in Land's *Letter to the Rev. Mr. Whitefield*, cited below, and written in 1737, though not published till 1739, a 'Deacon.' The breach between him and the Wesleys, into whose 'society' he had entered in 1735, and the consequent split among Methodists, was not declared till 1740–1.

Now, there is no indication of Whitefield's having, on the occasion of his visit to Manchester in December 1738, after his return from Georgia, preached in St. Ann's Square, or in any part of Manchester. But neither do we find this recorded of his subsequent visits to Manchester or the neighbourhood, to which Tyerman (N.S., vol. ii) assigns the following dates: 1749, 1752, 1753, 1755 and 1756. Mr. Axon, indeed (*Annals of Manchester*, p. 82) says that he preached twice in Manchester in 1739, viz., on December 3rd and 24th; but the earlier occasion must have been that of the two sermons at Salford (see quotation from *Diary* cited as above) and to the later date Mr. Axon appends a ?.

Thus, it seems on the whole safest to suppose that Whitefield must have preached in St. Ann's Square on the occasion of his visit in December 1738, and that it was about this time that the charges were brought against him by the *Manchester Magazine* (the title adopted in 1737 by *Whitworth's Manchester Gazette*) which are discussed

in the two pieces printed after the present. If it had
proved possible to unearth the number or numbers of
the *Magazine*, in which the scandal was circulated, the
question would have been set at rest. Land's letter, as
already observed, was published in 1739 (see *introductory note*
to the piece which I have entitled *Scandal against Whitefield*).

Byrom's general attitude towards Methodism is well known.
By natural disposition, as well as by the tendencies of his
religious thought, he stood nearer to men and women of the
'enthusiastic breed' proper, which even the founders of
Methodism professed to abhor—to the true descendants, that
is, of the medieval Mystics—than to the organised religious
revival of which the Wesleys were the beginners and in which
Whitefield and they were associated before the breach of
1740–1. But Whitefield had characteristics of his own which
found fuller expression in his subsequent career, and which
brought him nearer to Byrom than to the brothers; though
the earnestness and piety of the whole movement could not
fail to call forth a response in one who cherished a fervent
belief in Christianity and to whom nothing could be alien
that was inspired by Christian belief. The feeling against
the Methodists rose to its height with the anonymous publication of *Observations upon the Conduct and Behaviour of a
certain Sect, usually distinguished by the name of Methodists*
(1744), which was attributed to Dr. Edmund Gibson, Bishop
of London, and which was in part directed against Whitefield.

From ll. 37 to 43 of the present piece it may be conjectured
that it was addressed to Joseph Hoole, Rector of St. Ann's
from 1736 to 1745, and author of Sermons on several
important subjects (2 vols., 1741). He was a friend of
Byrom, and held non-juring opinions (cf. *Remains*, vol. i,
pp. 519 and 386, and notes).]

WELL, I have read your Sermon, Rev'rend Friend,
    Against the Methodists from end to end;
And, having heard it preach'd, you know, before,
With greater readiness have conn'd it o'er,

And now, sit down—to give without disguise
My thoughts upon it, just as they arise!
   First, then, I would observe that here you charge
Without distinction Methodists at large.
Not one of them but, by a gen'ral rule,
Must either be a Madman or a Fool,   10
Enthusiastic, bold, presumptuous, vain,
Or weak and ignorant, and lacking brain;
And all involv'd in one disastrous fate
Of being friends to neither Church nor State.
Now, this, I think, is only mere declaim,
With great aversion to a word, a name;
And, if not all, as one may hope, are such,
Nothing is prov'd by aiming at too much.
You only show them, by the names you call,
That you dislike 'em in the lump—that's all.   20
   "But," you may say—to treat that matter next,
"You know the man that made me chuse the text.
Did not I point sufficiently out
Him and his Hearers to exclude all doubt?"
Yes; yes—too plainly! That's the fault I find:
That your own gentle hearers have assigned
One of his own Ecclesiastic rank,

11. *Enthusiastic*. See Byrom's 'poetical essay, *Enthusiasm* (written 1752) and *prefatory note, ante*, vol. ii, pp. 167—197. Cf. the extract from an unpublished MS. note-book, mainly in Byrom's hand: 'September 14th, 17. From Dr. Hammond, which Mr. [Cattell ?] lent me, who preached yesterday against Enthusiasm, as he then thought, because of me.' (As to Cattell cf. *ante*, vol. i, p. 45 *note, et al.*) This must refer to an extract from Henry Hammond, as to whose tolerance see *ante*, vol. i, p. 353 note, and of whom Byrom was a great admirer. For the rest, as indicated above, John Wesley, in Overton's words (*The English Church in the Eighteenth Century*, p. 238), 'repeatedly and anxiously rebuts the charges of Enthusiasm which were levelled upon him from all sides.'

15. *Declaim*, declamation.
26. *Assigned*, designated.

I

A brother Clergyman, a Mountebank !
How could his text suggest the terms polite
Of "giddy populace" and "shocking sight"   30
Where order and where decency succeed,
We must extend to word as well as deed,
To speech and *all* alike their influence spread,
And all in word as well as deed be said.
  Next, then, of cries you give us a detail,
Which round the undiscerning mob prevail.
Now, granting, Sir, that all the Square were blind,
Granting your sight to be the most refin'd—
Blind people don't go wilfully astray :
Should you not lead them gently to their way?   40
If words of harshness stimulate the ear,
They will grow deaf, as well as blind, I fear;
They will be driven from the Church, and then
Surround in crowds the "Mountebank" again.
Why should you chuse, moreover, to reply
To what a Mob shall say, without an Eye?
Had you attack'd the Preacher, in their room,
Who had his eyes about him, I presume;
Had you expos'd what he himself held forth,
Your arguments had had their weight and worth,   50
The point in question properer dispatch,
Yourself at least a less unequal match.
But, since it was not regular to show
One pair of eyes among a whole blind crew;

28. *A brother Clergyman.* Whitefield was ordained in 1736.

34. This line cannot be said to be very clear, though the meaning may be guessed.

37. No doubt St. Ann's Square, Manchester, and below, l. 43, St. Ann's Church, where the sermon was probably preached. As to Whitefield's preaching in the Square, see *Introduction.* There seems to be an allusion here to 'Mountebank Green,' whose stage, as Byrom notes in *Remains,* vol. i, p. 40, was in 1722 set up in St. Ann's Square. (Cf. *ante,* vol. i, p. 368, and vol. ii, p. 650.)

46. A 'blind' mob.

Since you disdain'd to hear of one of School,
A Preacher standing only on a stool—
Th' Established Method was, it seems, preferr'd,
The Legal course, to answer him unheard.
    But, to consider, by your Sermon led,
"Not who it is that says, but what is said,"   60
They say—be who they will (tho', by the bye,
"They say," the Proverb says, "is half a lie)—
That such and such—and still no matter who—
Labour and Preach beyond what others do :
They Preach the Gospel freely, without gain,
And better than Established men explain.
This "they say" *gratis*, and, in answer, you
Tell us, for nothing, that they don't say true.
This really seems, the more one looks into 't,
The sum and substance of the whole Dispute.   70

55. Since you disdained to listen to a trained clergyman preaching in the open air. But it is difficult to feel sure as to the reading ' one of School.'

57. The irony of this line is more cutting than is usual with Byrom. The orthodox 'method' was held good enough by way of reply to the ' methodist.'

62. The proverb ' They say so, is half a lie ' is given, without indication of origin, in H. G. Bohn's *Handbook of Proverbs* (1857), p. 526.

WHITEFIELD IN THE SQUARE.

A DIALOGUE.

[As to Whitefield or Whitfield (the spelling of the transcript not being quite certain, what seems the correcter form of the name has been adopted) see *introductory note* to the preceding piece. Cf. as to Whitefield's own opinion of his gifts as a field-preacher, *note* to vol. ii, p. 190 *ante*.

It is curious to observe that, as already mentioned, John Wesley, who at first had disliked open-air preaching, as

carried on by Whitefield, himself adopted the practice, not
long after the return of the latter from Georgia and his visit
to Manchester, in the first instance at Bristol in April, 1739.

Concerning *The Manchester Magazine*, as *The Manchester
Gazette*, published by Henry Whitworth called itself from
1737, cf. *ante*, vol. i, p. 295. The number or numbers of
the *Magazine* to which reference is made in this and in the
succeeding piece have, as stated, not proved recoverable.]

[A.] YOUR hearing Whitfield in the Square offends
          Not without Reason, some of your good friends.
[B.] I'm sorry for 't. What is that Reason, pray?
      I'm not offended that they kept away.
      Better, according to my share of sense,
      Where judgments differ, not to take offence.
[A.] Why, 'tis encouraging, they seem to fear,
      That Stroller and his Mob, for you to hear
      The stuff and nonsense that he comes to broach—
[B.] This is not Reason, Neighbour, but Reproach.   10
      They have not heard him, nor has he heard them;
      Why should they be so eager to condemn?
[A.] But those that were at his Harangues, you find,
      Morning and Evening, are of the same mind.
[B.] What, all of them?
[A.]   No, I suppose that some
      By this delusive Talk were overcome.
[B.] Whose mind, then, do you mean?
[A.]   Why, you have seen,
      I make no Question, *Whitworth's Magazine?'*
[B.] Yes—but is this th' authority you join
      To strengthen that of these good Friends of mine?   20
      'Tis something marvellous, I own, to me
      How such extremes should happen to agree!
      Have Magazine accounts, then, been so just
      That you or they can take 'em upon trust,

18. *Whitworth's Magazine.* See *introductory note.*

Or think, tho' Whitefield may have faults eno',
The Bible and the Blanket story true?

[A.] That does, indeed, sound like a hearsay stretch,
Made by some poor calumniating wretch,
And, without proof, retail'd by this low spark,
Whose awkward zeal has overshot its mark.   30
But to false Doctrine—what d'ye say to that?
Fact, in this point, is easy to come at.

[B.] Before you call it false, come at it then!
Sunday, you know, he is to Preach again:
Whoever, therefore, can persuade his heart
To act the cautious, or the candid, part—
Let him forbear attendance, if he will,
And, not oblig'd, say neither good nor ill;
Or, if he will be judge in such a Cause,
Hear what deserves or Censure or Applause.   40

[A.] Why, I can't say but that is really fair:
I think, I'll go myself into the Square,
Since we are promis'd, if we chance to want,
An antidote to all his pois'nous rant.—
But now, in the meanwhile, pray, let me know
What's your opinion of the man?

[B.]   No, no!
You for yourself will judge as well as I
Of 'pois'nous' rant and 'antidote' reply.
Only, thro' Love or Hatred to a Sect,
Despise no Truth for any man's defect!   50
One thing I'll answer for: on Tuesday next,
With Poison and with Antidote Pretext,
You'll find (mark this Prediction, if you please)
The Remedy much worse than the Disease.

26. *The Bible and the Blanket* tolerably clear from the ensuing
story. The nature of the scandal piece, ll. 15-16.
charged against Whitefield is

SCANDAL AGAINST WHITEFIELD.

[It is uncertain to what 'pamphlet' the following lines refer. In the letter to his wife dated February 8th, 1739 (*Remains*, vol. ii. pp. 217–9), in which Byrom mentions Whitefield's visit to Manchester in the previous December, he says: 'The book against Mr. Whitfield by Mr. Land is thought a weak piece;—there is an answer supposed to [be] by a Quaker, or one under that character, not by Mr. Whitfield or any of his friends.' The full title of this precious production, of which a copy is preserved in the John Rylands Library, is: '*A Letter to the Rev. Mr. Whitefield, designed to correct his Mistaken Account of Regeneration, or the New Birth. Written before his Departure from London; then laid aside for some private Reasons; and now Published to prevent his doing Mischief among the Common People, upon his Return from Georgia. With a Previous Letter, addressed to the Religious Societies.* By Tristram Land, M.A., late Fellow of Clare Hall in Cambridge, Curate of St. James's, Garlick-hith, and Lecturer of the United Parishes of St. Anthony, and St. John Baptist, London, 1739.' The *Previous Letter*, which is a sort of preface to the attack proper, consists of a characteristic exposition of the grand argument that Methodism and the movement organised by it amount to 'an artificial Design of Satan,' which may be summarised as follows: 'To put Novices and New Beginners in the Spiritual Life, upon undertaking Severities more than they can bear, or greater than they can well go thro' with; with this Purpose you may be sure, that when they grow weary of them they may throw all Religion aside, together with their voluntary Usages, as too burthensome and not fit to be practised.' The letter to Whitefield himself inveighs against him for 'preaching up the Necessity of the New Birth, and thereby impugning the sufficiency of Regeneration by baptism'—to be supplemented, in the case of a falling away, by 'the several Means of Grace that are still offered towards Recovery and Amendment,' or, in one word, by a process of renewal through repentance.

Of course, it cannot be proved that this was the *opusculum* which had been sent to Byrom by 'friend Croxton.' Mr. Croxton, who appears (in June 1743) in a jovial mood (see *Remains*, vol. ii, p. 368), was no doubt a member of the old Cheshire family of Croxton, for many generations owners of the manor of Croxton near Middlewich, and afterwards of that of Ravenscroft (till 1704). He may have been the Mr. Croxton who, in 1725, purchased a house and lands at Guilden-Sutton, of which estate his grandson became owner in 1773 (see Lysons' *Cheshire*, pp. 690, 693, 787). Geoffrey Croxton was boroughreeve of Manchester 1639–40 (Axon, *Annals*, p. x).]

THIS Pamphlet that you sent me yesternight
   Tempts me, Friend Croxton, having read, to write.
Whitefield has made such talk here in the town,
Some so cry up his Preaching, some so down,
That one that fears to run into extremes
Can neither flatter nor condemn his schemes.
But, as I hate a false accusing spleen,
Such as appears in *Whitworth's Magazine*,
I will examine, and appeal to you,
Whether the Facts which he has lay'd are true.   10
   That Whitefield us'd expressions unpolite
Is but a trifling charge—perhaps, he might;
But that his fav'rite Doctrines are all prest
Into the Service of Self-Interest;
That, by his arts, the pois'nous Ranter got
Bibles and Blankets from the needy Scot—
This is such shocking Avarice and Gain

2. *Friend Croxton.* See intro-   15. Cf. *ante*, *Whitefield in the*
ductory note.   *Square*, l. 26.

As calls for proof beyond exception plain.
Such monstrous Witness, if 'tis false beside,
What Bible will excuse, what Blanket hide?   20
　　Now, ask the man who loads him with this guilt
What is the Evidence whereon 'tis built!
Was he himself in Scotland at the time
And, by some chance, Eye-witness to the Crime?
Was this ungodly and inhuman theft
Told him by any of the poor bereft?
Does Whitefield own it; or does Proof appear
Tho' he denies it, positive and clear?
In short, what reason does R. Whitworth bring
So soundly to assert so gross a thing?   30
—None in the world that, in a Court of Law,
Of Conscience either, signifies a straw.
Somebody, yonder at New England, writ
To his friend Somebody, a Glasgow Cit,
And gave accounts all true—if you suppose
That nothing false can come from Whitefield's foes.
Another Somebody, another foe,
Prints 'em—and this is all we are to know.
The gen'rous Author did, it seems, insist
That none should put his name into their list.   40
　　Previous to this anonymous Dispute,
There comes a Preface, with a Postscript to 't,
Wherein the unknown Editor affirms
(Of his false English if I guess the terms),
That one or two poor creatures had declar'd
That nothing but their Bibles could be spar'd,
And Whitefield, base and disingenuous, took,
As nothing else was to be had, the Book.

29. Robert Whitworth, the Manchester bookseller and publisher, whose business, according to *Remains*, vol. ii, p. 199, 'was not very lucrative, as he appeared in the *Gazette* as a bankrupt, February, 1738.'

35. There is, we know, great virtue in an *If*.

Charg'd, hereupon, with Bible theft alone—
'The Blanketts off their Beds' is Whitworth's own— 50
Special good Proof! So, still to make it better,
Read such a page and such of this same Letter!
Add, if you please, th' accuser's Christian skill:
He gives bad words—but out of mere good will;
All want of circumstance that should convince
His own opinion has supply'd long since.
Thus, having talk'd of present 'pois'nous Rant'
He scorns alike to instance, or recant;
Nay, owns—such social Courage what can damp?—
The Sermons *here* were of a diff'rent stamp. 60
    Should not his teachers, think ye, Sir, advise
Their pertinacious Pupil to be wise?
To let, with all the influence that he has,
Subjects above his understanding pass;
Not to conceit that printing public news,   ⎫
His private duty binds him to abuse--   ⎬
Not the effect of meaning, but of Use;   ⎭
Make him to give this necessary hint:
'Sirs, never mind the Scandal that I print?'

49. The construction is not clear here, and the punctuation must, consequently, be uncertain.

52. We should say : read page so and so.

55. All deficiencies in the way of circumstantial evidence.

67. This being the effect, not of bad intentions, but of a bad habit.

CHRISTIAN TRUTH AND THE REVIEWERS.

[What Reviewers of a Deistic or other heterodox tendency
can be in question here, by the title of whose journal the
monosyllabic blank in l. 12 could be filled up? Or is a mere
epithet in question, and could 'new,' or something of the
kind, serve the purpose? The Deistical movement had
certainly gone through every phase that could have suggested
a choice of epithets before it reached the point where all
controversy ceases.]

THEY who Believe, what is profest by most,
One God, one Father, Son and Holy Ghost,
Into Whose Name all Nations are appriz'd
That Christians are, by Christ's Command, Baptiz'd,
May well conceive, without Disputes jejune,
That God's all-perfect Nature is *Triune*;
May well reject the palpable extremes
Of Deist, Arian, Socinian schemes.
But, when pretence of Reason, Scripture, Sense
(Which is so often nothing but Pretence)   10
To Christian Truth has rais'd up wordy Foes,
Such as these————*Reviewers*, we'll suppose —
One may well question whether to descend
To monthly stagers serve to any end;
Whilst it appears that Sophistry will run
To some Excess that it has always done.
Th' undoubted Saints of ev'ry age agree
In One true Godhead of the Sacred Three—
Of Father, Word and Spirit; but, so weak
Is any human broken Speech to speak   20
Of this great Truth in Controversial way,
That very little sense can raise a Fray;

And the defects of language can produce
A world of terms for Controversy's use,
On ev'ry side, if some superior Grace
To apprehend shall not decide the case;
Where real Truth is of a deeper kind
Than words alone can fasten on the Mind.

23. This is almost better than the famous

Denn eben wo Gedanken fehlen,
Da stellt im Wort zu rechter
Zeit sich ein

in Goethe's *Faust;* for Byrom says that while human speech is unequal to the expression of a great truth, its very imperfections render it always fit for the expressions of half-truths or mere arguments.

LAW'S *APPEAL.*

[These kindly, but in part rather senile, lines seem to have been composed about the year 1751 or 1752 (see l. 24, and cf. *note* to l. 27), *i.e.*, in Byrom's sixtieth or sixty-first year. The 'Mr. Hooke' to whom they are addressed must have been John Hooke, a Hertfordshire clergyman, formerly of Trinity College, Cambridge, who is mentioned in *Remains*, vol. ii, p. 282, *s.a.* 1637, as about to teach Charles Wesley the art of shorthand, which Hooke had doubtless learnt from Byrom.

The celebrated Selina Countess of Huntingdon, afterwards the friend of Whitefield, Byrom, in 1735 (*Remains*, vol. i, pp. 592 and 610), speaks of having seen once and not again; in 1744, she expressed a strong wish that he should spend some time with her (*ib.*, vol. ii, p. 382); and, in 1761, he records a visit from John Wesley, who said that Lady Huntingdon 'was ill, and a more charming woman than ever; that she is the lady to whom Mr. Law wrote the letters in his book' (*ib.*, p. 629). The letters are, no doubt, the three (viii–x) addressed *To a Person of Quality* in vol. v of Law's *Works* (1769). As to Lady Huntingdon's extraordinary zeal in promoting the Evangelical Revival, more especially in the sphere of her own class, and as to the success of her efforts in London, Brighton, Bath and elsewhere, see Abbey and Overton, *The English Church in the Eighteenth Century,* new edn., pp. 347 *sqq.* The 'Connexion' called by her name at first cooperated with the Church; but, ultimately, those parish clergymen who had acted with her withdrew from the 'Connexion,' although still maintaining relations of personal intimacy with Lady Huntingdon herself. The ample account of her *Life and Times* published in two vols., in 1839, contains only a few references to Law; though she had become acquainted with Miss Hester Gibbon and her friend Mrs. Hutcheson, to both of whom Law was 'chaplain, instructor and almoner' at King's Cliffe soon after their settlement there. As to Law's *Appeal,* cf. *introductory note* to the lines *On the Fall of Man,* part ii, *ante.*]

DEAR Mr. Hooke,
        In taking up the Quill,
To answer yours, receiv'd from Clifton Hill,
I must begin the matter, where you end,
With the same Postscript, touching an old Friend.
Postscript—and by Commission, too—assures:
'Your old Acquaintance is *in Heart* much yours,'
  Thank you for this incomparable line!
God bless her Heart! for she rejoices mine
By her Commission to ye. For my part,
I love a native Honesty of Heart,   10
Such as my Lady Huntingdon, I guess'd,
When happy to converse with her, possess'd.
Her lovely, sharp Discernment of the True,
With Caution arm'd against Excesses, too,
Free, gen'rous, open, cordial, and sincere,
To what was right still prompted to adhere;
The love of Truth, the Substance, and the Root,

2. 'Early in the month of March (1751) Lady Huntingdon and family left Ashby for Bristol.' *The Life and Times of Selina, Countess of Huntingdon* (1839), vol. i, p. 171.
16. *Still,* ever.

Sav'd her from all the Cavils of Dispute ;
In various sentiments, the main affair,
However worded, seem'd to be her care ;   20
Whilst Judgment, fix'd upon its solid base
Rose to the summit, with each softer grace.
   To Cookham now ! The Clifton Lady saw
Excellent things in this *Appeal* of Law,
Where you—a Genius masculine—have found
A set of knotty Queries to propound ;
And many more, by your account I find,
The Difficulties that remain behind.
   O Friend ! O Mystic ! Is it thus that you,
In search of Truth, mere puzzlement pursue ?   30
This Book desir'd but one fair reading o'er,
And—as you think—you read it with two more,
When, just come forth, it fell into your hand
(Twelve years ago), and did not understand.
'Have it not by you !' Nothing now remains
But Difficulties, to reward your pains—
'Diff'rence of Disposition among Friends !'
I must digress, to make myself amends
For their repugnance to a fav'rite page,
Meant, as I deem, a Blessing to an Age,   40
And hear what Memory suggests of one
Who at that time thought otherwise thereon :
Honest JACOBI—German, and the Clerk
Of Chapel somewhere by St. James's Park.

23. Cookham near Maidenhead, where the historian of Rome, Nathaniel Hooke, the life-long friend of Pope, died in 1763. He is described by Warburton, cited in *Dict. of Nat. Biog.*, vol. xxvii, as ' a mystic and quietist, and a warm disciple of Féne-lon '; and he seems to have had Roman Catholic sympathies.

Byrom's friend must have been a kinsman of his.

27. The *Appeal*, as is noted below, appeared in 1740.

43. As to Johann Christian Jacobi, a German pietist and Keeper of the German Chapel Royal in St. James's Palace, see *ante*, vol. ii, pp. 99—100, and *ib.*, p. 87, for references to *Remains*.

My Lady Huntingdon, I fancy, knew
The good old Man—his good old Manners, too.
I went to see him once, when he had lain
Upon his Bed, to mitigate his pain
From Stone to Gravel, for he could not sit
While then attack'd with a severer fit :   50
Upon a Chair, just by him, lay a Book;
And, asking what it was, he bade me look.
'Twas Law's *Appeal,* which somebody had been
Just reading to him, as I enter'd in—
Office to which he ask'd me to succeed;
Sent out the Person, and would have me read;
Pointed, by turns, to Passage and to Page,
To such good *Extracts* as could *Pains* assuage—
Fast, as the Feeler did himself declare,
For the dear Author putting up his Pray'r :   60
'Read that again—and that—for I am sure
Or not to feel, or patient to endure.
God's Name be prais'd, and Will submitted to !
How comfortable This ! how Just ! how True !'

THE DOGMA OF REPROBATION.

[The following lines clearly have reference to some stage of the Calvinistic controversy—and, of course, to one earlier than the last and most important stage, which began in 1770-1, after Byrom's death. The controversy originally broke out in a correspondence between Wesley and Whitefield in 1739-40, during Whitefield's absence in America, in which the latter took up the strictly Calvinistic position on the subject of Predestination. (See, as to his attitude towards Wesley, the touching letter *ap.* Tyerman, *Life of Whitefield*, vol. i, pp. 389-90.) A rupture between them ensued early in 1741 (*ib.*, p. 475). Although their personal friendship was reestablished in the autumn of 1742, the first Conference of Calvinistic Methodists was held in January 1743, and the second, at which Whitefield was chosen Perpetual Moderator of the General Association, in April following. It would appear to be to these proceedings (of which an account will be found in Tyerman, vol. ii, pp. 49 *sqq.*) and their result that the first lines of the present piece refer; but it should be noted that Whitefield agreed with Wesley in deprecating any separation of their respective Societies from the Church. (*Ib.*, vol. ii, p. 70.) After the Calvinistic controversy had more or less subsided, it was revived by the publication of James Hervey's *Theron and Aspasia* in 1755. In this book, the Calvinistic doctrine of Imputed Righteousness was maintained in a style which, like that of the author's earlier *Meditations and Reflections*, proved hightly attractive to the 'general reader.' (See as to *Theron and Aspasia*, and Wesley's *Remarks* on the book, Introductory note to Byrom's *Thoughts on Imputed Righteousness*, vol. ii, pp. 482 *seqq., ante.*) Byrom, as a follower of Law, was fundamentally opposed to the teaching of Calvinism which inspired these modern 'Covenanters' as it had the old. (Cf., as to the general course of the Calvinistic controversy, Abbey and Overton's *English Church in the Eighteenth Century*, pp. 355 *sqq.*)]

THESE People promise, by a formal Deed,
    God, and each other, to maintain a Creed,
Which, on a calm, unprejudic'd Review,
All sober sense would show them was not true
In ev'ry [part]—particularly one
Where Reprobation is insisted on.
Do they reflect what 'Reprobation' means?
The Complication of all horrid Scenes,
Of all the Torments of the Damn'd in Hell—
Endless, immense! If they consider'd well,   10
Could they believe that an Abyss of Ill
Was fix'd by righteous Council of God's Will;
That this Damnation was a glorious End,
Which He, from everlasting, would intend?
That the Almighty's Holiness and Power
Could will an Hell, His creatures to devour;
That Allsufficiency could want to raise,
From this eternal Misery, a Praise;
That men were made, by God's own Reprobation,
Objects of hatred, prior to Creation?—   20
These, and the like Positions of this kind,
Shock the [plain] Sense of ev'ry sober mind;
And yet all these, in most expressive terms,
Their Creed, in Article the Fourth, affirms:
Not one of which, till Times began to fall

22. *Transcript*: Shock the Sense.

7. ' You must formally recant the *abominable doctrine* of reprobation, so contrary to sound reason, and then preach only *free grace* in the blood of the Lamb, and an *election of Grace* as taught in the Scriptures . . . and if not, our Church must necessarily be opposed to you.' *Count Zinzendorf to Whitefield* (1743). (Tyerman, vol. ii, p. 68.)

From Christian Faith, was ever broach'd at all.
Amongst the num'rous Heresies of old
One hears of none that ever was so bold
As to advance such Principles as here
These Covenanters take to be so clear,   30
And promise God to stand by; Tho' his Will
That none should perish be in Scripture still—
To such Excess, in all appearance, led
By some Men's Talk, or Books which they have read.
Of famous Leaders in some modern Sect,
For whom conceiving a well-meant Respect,
They took such Notions from these Heads alone
As never should have come into their own.
     For how could they, whilst honest and untaught,
Have entertain'd so desperate a Thought   40
As to suppose, that ever God design'd—
The God of Love—to reprobate Mankind,
Or any part of them—the greatest part,

24. According to J. B. Figgis, *The Countess of Huntingdon and her Connexion* (1891), pp. 47-50, the Articles of Religion, "the bond which still unites the ministers and the congregations" of the Connexion, were drawn up at a date soon after her secession from the Church of England (1781) by those of the ministers that had worked with her who had "gone the full length and seceded also." But these articles must, at least in part, have been settled earlier, as the Article IV of the Fall of Man from Original Righteousness, which is evidently that to which Byrom refers, runs as follows: "Our first parents sinned, in eating the forbidden fruit; whereby they fell from their original righteousness, and became wholly defiled in all the faculties and parts of soul and body. And, being the root of all mankind, the guilt of this sin was imputed, and the same corrupted nature conveyed to all their posterity descending from them, by ordinary generation."

30. The Calvinistic Methodists held their first 'Association' eighteen months before Wesley held his first Methodist Conference in London (Tyerman, *Life of Whitefield*, vol. ii, p. 50); so that, apart from their tenets, the former had a primary claim to be called the new 'Covenanters.'

As they pretended who began to start
Th' unheard-of doctrine of a God most good,
Appointing Reprobates because He would;
Bounding His own Prerogative to bless;
To greater good preferring to do less;
Rejecting many, and receiving few,
Tho' all alike, to show what He could do !　　50
Dooming to endless Misery and Scorn
Innumerable children yet unborn,
To show His Pow'r—as if it wanted show
From any Creature's predetermined Woe;
Giving commands to all, which only they
Who cannot help obeying can obey;
Promising Good, by His revealèd Will,
And, by His secret, preordaining Ill !
No end of monstrous Maxims that ensue,
When such an Article is held for true　　60
As makes a God so acting as, in case
Of human Fathers, would infer Disgrace
On all parental characters, in fine,
Reversing ev'ry attribute Divine,
Ev'ry Description of His gracious Aid,
Who 'hateth nothing that Himself hath made.'
　Some who set up their Reprobating plan
Made it posterior to the Fall of Man.
Damnation's Misery, they all agreed,
But for some Sin, should never be decreed ;　　70
All being seen involv'd in Adam's Guilt,
Then, the Discriminating Plan was built,
And God ordain'd—according to their Faith—
Vessels of Mercy some, and some of Wrath;
So Sublapsarians, as they call them, say,

66. 'Almighty and Everlasting
God, who hatest nothing that
Thou hast made.' *Collect for
Ash Wednesday.*

75. *Sublapsarians.* Those who
hold that God permitted the Fall
without ordaining it.

Whose system passes for the mod'rate way—
Tho', in effect, the Diff'rence is but small,
While God is made not willing to save all.
   This Paper, pushing to the last extreme
The most horrendous Reprobating scheme,   80
Will have no Sin to intervene between
Damning Decree, committed or foreseen.
Men were rejected, reprobated, curst,
And fitted for Destruction, from the first—
Objects of God's unutterable Hate,
Even before it pleas'd Him to create;
Consign'd to everlasting Wrath, to dwell
With Devils, and with Spirits damn'd in Hell.
Supralapsarian System this, the Case
Which these, so far deluded, Souls embrace.   90
   Now, tho' an Error of enormous kind
May not be always willful, or design'd,
Because some Persons, taught it from their youth,
May take it, all unwittingly, for Truth—
Yet, as it brings upon the Christian Name
Scandal as great as words alone can frame,
Whilst it derives the Origin of Ill
From God's Decree, instead of Man's Selfwill—
Compendious Article, to overthrow
All Reason, Law, and Gospel, at a blow—   100
From such an Error, in the least Degree
Who would not wish his Neighbours to be free?

89. *Supralapsarian System.* the Fall was predestined by God
The belief of those who hold that from all eternity.

MOSES'S PRINCIPIA.

[Of the Hutchinsonian tenets, towards which Byrom here, as became him, takes up a gently sceptical attitude—probably intended to calm the eagerness of some would-be follower of the new sect, a sufficient account will be found in Sir Leslie Stephen's *English Thought in the Eighteenth Century*, vol. i, pp. 389–392 (where reference is made to R. Shearman's *Life of Hutchinson*), and a briefer summary in the same writer's article *Hutchinson, John*, in vol. xxviii of the *Dictionary of National Biography*. The Hutchinsonian school represents a reaction against rationalism, which took the form of an attempt to refute Newton's theory of gravitation by means of symbolical interpretation of the Book of Genesis, and to reconcile Geology and Scripture, the just relations between were held to have been recently called into question. To Hutchinson's chief work, *Moses's Principia* (2 parts, 1724-7, reference was made above (p. 101). It is not a book for ordinary readers. Hebrew words expressing spiritual things are, all of them, treated in it as, in each case, taking their significance from created materials, though often only indicating degrees or branches of the whole which they express. This treatment is applied in the case of successive verses of the first chapter of *Genesis*, with the aid of notes containing an enormous mass of illustrative matter. (See, as an example, the notes on the sentence : 'And the Spirit of God moved on the Face of the Waters.') 'My intention,' says the writer incidentally, 'is no other but to make the Scripture intelligible, which has no difficulties in these Points, but what has been made by Philosophers.' 'He found,' says Sir Leslie Stephen, 'a number of symbolic meanings in the Bible and in nature, and thought, for example, that the union of fire, light and air was analogous to the Trinity. Among his followers were Bishop Horne, Jones of Nayland, and Julius Bate, the last named of whom Hutchinson appointed to the rectory of Sutton, of which the Duke of Somerset had given him the presentation. Bate, author of *Critica Hebræa, or a Hebrew-English Dictionary without points* (1767) bravely involved himself in a quarrel with Warburton on behalf of the school.

The doubt suggested in these verses as to the positive value of hieroglyphical interpretations, however, confidently advanced, suggests a passage in Law's *Defence of Enthusiasm* (cited by Norton, *William Law*, p. 309) : of 'He whose heated brain is all over painted with the ancient hieroglyptics; who knows how and why they were this and that, better than he can find out the customs and usages of his own parish; who can clear up everything that is doubtful in antiquity, &c., &c., may well despise those Christians, as brain-sick visionaries, who are sometimes finding a moral and spiritual sense in the bare letter and history of Scripture facts. . . .']

I.

THE Hieroglyphic Figure, and the Oath,
　Or Curse, implied, have such appearance both
As does not tend at all to reconcile
One's thinking mind to Hutchinsonian style,
But breaths a Doubt, that this new Hebrew plan
Wants to go further than it really can.

II.

This instituted Emblem stood, of old,
To represent the Greek Ones, we are told;
That is, the Persons of the Sacred Three,
As Model Patterns, far as it could be;   10
And the same phrase for the Material Sign
Was us'd as for th' Invisible, Divine.

III.

It was the only Book, from Adam's Fall,
Scripture entire—in other words, for all:

5. *Breaths,* breathes.

Not them alone of Patriarchal race,
But all the Heathen world, in ev'ry place,
Before the use of letters was made known,
To Moses first, by Revelation, shown.

IV.

Some figure, spoken of with so much awe,
Contain'd the substance of the Written Law,   20
And, what is still more marvellous to tell
Of such a Book, was understood, as well,
The Faith and Duty of a Christian, too,
Entire—what will not Hieroglyphics do!

V.

The Compact, Oath, Ban, Execration, Curse,
Which it refers to, seems to be still worse,
If Doctor Sharp, *On Elohim*, recite,
The various terms of his opponents right.
But one suspends, till seen along with him,
The learned Bate *Upon the Cherubim*.   30

VI

Meanwhile, if anyone will touch the Theme
Who understands the Hutchinsonian Scheme,
And place it in a plainer, cooler view
Than here the learnèd Rabbins chose to do,
Fondness for Hebrew will engage to pay
The due Regard to all that he shall say.

34. *Transcript*: Gittins. Rabbins, *conj.*

27. Dr. Thomas Sharp published in 1751, *Two Dissertations concerning the Etymology and Scripture-meaning of the Hebrew words Elohim and Berith*, which criticised the 'notions' of Hutchinson and A. Calcott. Among the replies to Sharp was one by Julius Bate; and, in 1755, Sharp published *Mr. Hutchinson's Exposition of Cherubim, and his Hypothesis concerning them Examined.*

34. The conjecture ' Rabbins ' seems obvious. ' Gittins,' a Hebrew word signifying ' bills of divorcement,' makes no sense here.

WESLEY ON LAW.

[The following two pieces, whose relation to each other as part i and part ii (see ll. 35–6 and note) seems beyond doubt must have been written before 1756. The 'neighbour' (part i, l. 7) to whom they were addressed is unknown. The clue to their intention is furnished by a passage in the late Canon Overton's *William Law, Non-juror and Mystic* (1881), pp. 382–4—a work for which, as for much other light thrown on English religious history by this always interesting and never pretentious writer, a deep debt is due to him. The passage is worth quoting in full, or nearly so:

The last correspondence between Law and Wesley took place in 1738. After this they appear to have gone on their respective ways, holding no intercourse with one another. But, in 1756, Wesley, after eighteen years' silence, felt bound to give expression to his disappointment at Law's more pronounced development of mysticism, especially as it appeared in *The Spirit of Prayer* and *The Spirit of Love*.[1] This he did in the form of a letter or pamphlet [dated January 6th, 1756] addressed to Mr. Law,[2] but published for the benefit of Christians generally. (Reprinted in Wesley's *Works*, vol. IX.[3]) This pamphlet has been very severely condemned. Whitefield characterised it to Lady Huntingdon as 'a most unchristian and ungentlemanly letter.' Dr. Byrom on more than one occasion (August 1, 1757, and April 2, 1761,[4]) roundly took Wesley

1. *The Spirit of Prayer, or The Soul Rising out of the Vanity of Time into the Region of Eternity.* In two parts, part i, 1749; part ii, 1750, in three *Dialogues;* and *The Spirit of Love,* part i, 1752, in a *Letter to a Friend,* part ii, 1754, in three *Dialogues.*

2. *A Letter to the Rev. Mr. Law, occasioned by some of his Writings.* By John Wesley, A.M., 1756.

3. pp. 182—256, as an extract of *A Letter,* etc. Cf. Wesley's *Journal,* July 27th, 1749; edn. of 1827, vol. iii, p. 18.

4. Cf. *Remains,* vol. ii, pp. 593 and 599; and *ib.,* pp. 629—30.

to task, urging him to ' repent of that wicked letter,' and on
Wesley's promise to soften some of his expressions about Law,
quoted the line :—

Multæ non possunt, una litura potest.

But the letter was not ' wicked,' nor ' unchristian,' nor ' ungentlemanly,' nor did it deserve the ' *una litura,*' the entire obliteration,
which Byrom suggested. From Wesley's own point of view it was
a very natural one; and it was written, like everything that was
written by that great and good man, from the purest motives; nor
is it difficult to see what those motives were. To do reasonable
justice to Wesley we must remember that he was an eminently
practical man . . . . . Hence this well-meant, if not very judicious,
attempt to counteract the evil. Law characterised it (in a private
letter, however, not intended for publication) in his own incisive
language, as ' a juvenile composition of emptiness and pertness,
below the character of any man who had been serious in religion but
half a month.'[1] (See also Letter ix, dated Feb. 16, 1756, in vol.
v. of Law's *Works.*) 'And regarding it purely as an intellectual
performance, perhaps Law was not very far wrong. Wesley had
obviously a very imperfect acquaintance with Behmenism. While
condemning Law, he strongly praised Byrom's poems, which are
really nothing more than a reproduction of Law in verse; and he
actually reprinted for the use of his disciples Law's answer to
Warburton, which is Behmenish to the very core, evidently not
detecting the Behmenism which it contained. The fact is, such
speculations were entirely out of Wesley's line, and in this pamphlet he laid himself open to a crushing retort which no one could
have administered more effectually than Law. But Law was not
the man to do it. Men who write from obviously Christian motives
were not the men whom Law ever chose to attack. ' Wish them
well in all that is good,' was his advice to a friend who censured
the Methodists, in reference to this very pamphlet. This was the
reason—and not as Wesley supposed, contempt for the writer—
which kept Law silent. See for an austere though not ingenious
condemnation of the *The Spirit of Prayer* Wesley's *Journal*, July
27th, 1749; and cf, as to the change in Wesley's attitude towards
Law, the Letter of the former to the Editor of the *London Chronicle,*
September 17th, 1760].

1. Wesley's *Journal*, Sept. 17, 1760, edn. 1827.

PART I.

THESE pious Tracts that Wesley takes in hand
  And thus condemns—he does not understand;
Things in themselves so excellent and good
How could he censure, if he understood?
Of all the grievous faults which he has found
Zeal beyond Judgment is the only ground.
Since you desire me, Neighbour, to express
My thoughts on reading, what can one say less?
A Letter fill'd with so unjust a blame
Will gain few Converts to the Writer's fame.   10
That full Conviction which the Books, when read,
Afford of Truth, in what the Author said,
Momentous, Christian, comfortable, plain,
Seen all along its own connected chain
Of Nature, Scripture, happily combin'd
To banish Doubt from an attentive Mind,
Cannot so readily be overthrown,
If once the Mind has made the Proof its own.
Easy to dip in Pages of a Book
And give to Query a perplexing look,   20
And give to such as never read them thro'
Of frightful Errors a forbidding view!
Easy, for men of learning and of wit,
To give a turn to Text of Holy Writ,
And then apply to make it contradict
An unconnected passage that is pickt.
Spread thus abroad is many a mistake
Which Writers teach their Readers how to make!
But, in the case of this mistake, the Grief
From Wesley's Letters may have this relief: 30
Its very vehemence may help to draw
Some searching people to examine Law,
To read his Doctrines, in his own *Appeal*,
And quash th' Indictment of the judging Zeal.

That Book, in which his whole Design appears,
Has been in print above these thirteen years
By one unnotic'd in a letter'd strain,
Who ' would not speak, but Dares not to refrain';
And other Books, all tending to evince
The same conclusions, have been publish'd since—   40
'*Some dreadful Mischief,*' in this Writer's style—
But yet produc'd no Letter, all the while.
Last, after all the Treatises devout,
That upon *Pray'r,* and that on *Love,* came out,
On which a fearful Zeal, the next still past,
Employ'd the Christmas Holy days at last.
      Now, after daring to refrain so long,
Surely, beginning at the End was wrong.
To hunt for Queries these two pieces o'er,
Without Regard to aught laid down before,   50
Looks rather like the Purpose of a Mind
In quest of Meanings which it wants to find,
Than such impartial Search to find the true
As fair Enquirers after Truth pursue,

35. *An appeal to all that Doubt or Disbelieve the Truths of the Gospel,* and characterised by Law's biographer as ' one of the most comprehensive and important of all his mystic works,' appeared in 1740, and is reprinted in vol. v. of Law's *Works.* This was sixteen (not thirteen) years before the appearance of Wesley's *Letters,* and before Byrom's lines could have been written.

37. Unnoticed in his writings by one.

38. See *Letter* : ' I do not undertake formally to refute what you have asserted in any of these heads. I dare not.'

39. *Other books.* It does not appear that any work of importance was published by Law between the *Appeal* and *The Spirit of Prayer.*

41. See *Letter* : ' I could not have borne to spend so many words on so egregious trifles, but that they are mischievous trifles.'

49. *To hunt for Queries.* This alludes to the method of Wesley's *Letter to Law* : ' I shall only give a sketch of this strange system, *and ask a few obvious questions.*'

Who judge of Writings by the real End
To which the whole of their Expressions tend—
Or true or false, observe what one may call
The first, the chief, the central Point of all.
This, in the Writings here by Wesley blam'd
And all the rest, has been so often nam'd   60
That none can doubt the Centre of their Plan,
The Love of God to his fall'n Creature, Man.
From this one Principle, so just and true,
So universally acknowledg'd, too,
Mankind's Redemption is display'd to sight,
In its most native amiable light :
As pure effect, when rightly understood,
Of God's unchang'd, eternal Will to Good,
Which nothing can prevent but Human Will,
Bent against Love, and full inclin'd to Ill.   70
 All Nature's volume, that of Books Divine,
All true Philosophy and Reason, join
To prove, or, rather, simply to declare,
What wants no Proof with men of *Love* and *Pray'r* :
That, to obtain Redemption from the Fall,
God's Love to us, and Ours to Him, is all;
Which this one Proof remains for us to make,
To love our Neighbour, purely for His sake;
That Love can only manifest its Pow'rs
Through CHRIST, the Centre of His Love and Ours,   80
In Whom all possible Perfections shine
Through Nature's Medium, Human and Divine.
In Truth so plain whoever seeks to raise
Objection can but do it to the Phrase;

57. Who, whether these be true or false, direct their attention to.

62. See especially the opening part of *The Spirit of Love.*

68. See *ib.* : ' This is the *one eternal immutable* God, that from Eternity to Eternity changes not, that can be neither more nor less, nor anything else, but an *eternal Will to all the Goodness* that is in himself, and can come from him.'

Can but allure us, by what hints he brings,
To dwell on Words and lose the sight of Things.
One Query serves for seeking things above :
'Does it increase, or does it lessen, Love ?'
For, by the Saviour's Word, to this one end
The Law, the Prophets, and the Gospel, tend;   90
By Love to God and Man, sincerely will'd,
Pray'd for, and granted, they are all fulfill'd.
Law, once, as Wesley says, exprest it thus,
That 'We love Him, because He first lov'd us';
Suggesting to him, when he was a youth,
The simple plainness of Religious Truth.
This he would hint that Law had since forgot,
And quotes the Tracts, which show that he has not.
The Truth is Gospel—be it, then, the Test
Of ev'ry Writing which explains it best.   100

90. See *St. Matthew*, ch. vii, v. 12. (Cf. the lines *post*, to which I have ventured to give the heading ' *The Law, the Prophets and the Gospel.*' ·

94. See Wesley's *Letter, ad. in.* : 'At a time when I was in great danger of not valuing this authority [that of Holy Writ] enough, you make that important observation : " I see where your mistake lies. You would have a philosophical religion ; but there can be no such thing. Religion is the most plain, simple thing in the world. It is only, *We love Him, because He first loved us*. So far as you add philosophy to religion, just so far you spoil it." This remark I have never forgotten since. And I trust in God, I never shall.' ' It is true,' writes Wesley in 1760, 'that Mr. Law, whom I love and reverence now, was once an oracle to me.' (*Journal, u.s.*, vol. iii, p. 19.)

PART II.

The Text of the belov'd Disciple, John,
That WESLEY seems to rest his charge upon,
That seems to introduce it, and, at last,
Concludes his Letter, after all had past,
Is made the Test of Truth denied or shown
In Tracts condemn'd, because it is his own.
The Meaning of it, undisputed, too,
Makes it a proper Test of false or true.
If any Sentiment, in either Tract,
Is inconsistent with the Text, in fact,   10
It merits condemnation; but, if not,
Then it must fall to be the Letter's Lot,
Which brings it in, as one may well distrust,
With more of artful consequence than just.
For, mark the notions which the Writer nurs'd,
When LAW made use of the expression first :
He did not value, in his younger age,
Th' authority enough of Scripture page;
He had then got (his Friend perceiv'd it, too)
Some kind of a *Philosophy* in view—   20
What, is not mention'd; but it did, you see,
With disregarded Scripture not agree.
Therefore, to such Philosophy as that,
Remark then made might possibly be pat,
That, in proportion as it was annex'd,

1. ' We love Him, because He first loved us.' 1 *Epistle of St. John*, ch. iv, v. 19. (*See the following note.*)

3. Wesley's *Letter* concludes with an admonition to Law to ' speak out of your mouth and out of your heart that *vain philosophy*, and *speak* neither higher nor lower things, neither more nor less than *the oracles of God*; to renounce, despise, abhor all the high flown bombast, all the unintelligible jargon of the mystics, and come back to the plain religion of the bible, *We love Him, because He first loved us*.'

It spoil'd the plain Religion of the Text,
And the Remarker's meaning might be clear
From Inconsistency suggested here.
Caution against Philosophy, you know,
Was given by an Apostle long ago—   30
Philosophy, of vain, deceitful kind,
After the world, not after Christ, defin'd;
For that which look'd on 'Christ as All in All'
Is recommended highly by Saint Paul,
In very mystic terms, which all assign
The true Philosophy of Love Divine.
And WESLEY, deeming of these Tracts amiss,
Has never shown that they depart from *this*.
    If they do not—if still it be the aim
Of that Philosophy which bears the Blame   40
To show this Love in ev'ry lovely view;
To prove, by Nature, Scripture to be true;
By ev'ry fitness that there can but be
One true *Redeemer*, and that *Christ* is He;
Tho' such hard words the Letter has bestow'd
On Proof of *Love*, in Philosophic Mode—
All can but come to this, which one may grant:
That they are needless, where there is no want.
LAW would be glad, if either you or I,
Having the Thing, could pass the Reasons by;   50
Which are but meant as written *Helps* to bring
A man to Pray, and to obtain the Thing—
The Blessèd Love, which God first showed to Men,

30. *Colossians,* ch. ii, vv. 8-9 : ' Beware lest any man spoil you through philosophy and vain deceit, after the tradition of men, after the rudiments of the world, and not after Christ. For in Him dwelleth all the fulness of the Godhead bodily.'

33. *Colossians,* ch. iv, vv. 10- 11 : 'And have put on the new man, which is renewed in knowledge after the image of him that created him : Where there is neither Greek nor Jew . . . . bond nor free : but Christ is all, and in all.'

35. *Assign,* declare.

The Cause, in them, of loving Him again.
To this, the final words of the attack ·
Upon his Book exhort him to come back;
When, on perusal, not a single word
In all their pages even once occurr'd,
Where he was charg'd with going from the Place
Which he is thus exhorted to retrace—   60
Not the least Query, not the least pretence
From either Tract, or its misconstrued sense,
Of having left what could afford a rise
To this conclusive coming-back advice,
Not possible to follow, you perceive;
For how 'come back' to what he did not leave?
If he had.left, the forwardness to find
So much objection of another kind,
So many Points which, if suppos'd, implied
That *Pow'r* in God, that Justice was denied,   70
Would have found some, in turning over Print,
Where *Love* receiv'd the like injurious hint:
Something to lessen, or but ill befriend
The Text, the Standard, at the Letter's end;
To give a just occasion to remind
Of 'coming back' to what was left behind;
But not a word of *Love* denied, the main
And central Point, does any page contain.
The wond'rous Fault that strikes a Reader's eye
Is raising up God's Love to us too high,   80
Denying in His Deity the Wrath
Which WESLEY takes for Article of Faith,

56. See note to l. 3 *above*.

60. *Retrace*, recover, return to.

64. That could supply a reason for the categorical exhortation (l. 56 *ante*).

82. 'As nothing,' writes Wesley, ' is more frequently or more expressly declared in Scripture, than God's anger at Sin, and his *punishing* it both temporarily and eternally, every assertion of this kind ' [that there is no eternal punishment, and in truth no punishment at all] ' strikes directly at the credit of the whole revelation.'

Inserting, out of Concordancial Store
Of Scripture Phrases, forty texts and more,
From the Old Testament and from the New,
A specious Comment upon one or two;
Before and after which, is amply shown
The sad Philosophy of Love alone.
   If you suppose the Letter to be writ
For any single purpose, this is it.   90
Now, whether right conception would define
Or Love, or Wrath, or both, to be Divine—
Let them exclude each other, or imply—
The Text insisted on whose Works deny?
Some good advice, for plain Religion's sake,
Both Writers give; which of them here should take?
As *Love* is, plainly, the forsaken Track,
The Wrath-asserter only can 'come back';
Right of *Recall* to 'We love Him, because
He first lov'd us' undoubtedly is LAW's.   100

83. A rather cruel allusion to a kind of 'index-learning' which neither controversial nor most other kinds of theological writing can easily spare.

84. They actually number forty-two.

88. *Sad,* bad. As we say 'a sad blunder.' (Johnson cites 'a sad husband.')

94. Whose writings contravene the text on which Wesley insists? (See ll. 1-2, *ante.*)

95—100. The concluding judgment, like some other judicial deliverances, requires a little study before its meaning becomes clear. Both Law and Wesley *give* some good advice— which of them should *take* it? Manifestly, Wesley is the one to come back to the Gospel of Love, and Law is entitled to recall him to it.

THE GOD-MAN.

TRANSLATION OF A LATIN EPIGRAM :

ESSE HOMINEM TANTUM, ETC.

[The original has not proved discoverable.]

WHEN they who think that Jesus is but MAN
Shall learn to live as like Him as they can ;
When they who think that He is GOD shall pay
Their Worship to Him in a godly way :
Both, by an inward proof, will come to find
JESUS—GOD—MAN—the Saviour of Mankind.

THE LAW, THE PROPHETS, AND THE GOSPEL.

'Whatsoever ye would that Men should do to you, do ye even so to them; for this is the Law and the Prophets.' *St. Matthew*, chap. vii, v. 12.

BEHOLD Religion in an easy View,
Which Self-Conviction teaches to be true :
'What ye desire that men should do to you
Do ye to them, for this is mutual Due;
This is the Testament, both Old and New,
The Law, the Prophets, and the Gospel, too.'

1. *In an easy View* : according to a definition as to which there can be no difficulty.

2. *Self-conviction* : the result of self-examination.

K

APPENDIX. I.

UNPUBLISHED LETTERS FROM JOHN BYROM TO JOHN STANS-
FIELD, AND FROM FRANCIS HOOPER TO JOHN BYROM.

[The MSS. of the following two series of letters are preserved in the Chetham Library, and have hitherto remained unprinted. Some time before the lamented death, in 1888, of the late John Eglington Bailey, F.S.A., the biographer of Fuller and for six years Honorary Secretary of the Chetham Society, it had been intended to publish these letters as Supplementary to Byrom's *Remains*, and Mr. Bailey had begun annotating them, besides prefixing some introductory remarks to the second series. His notes and observations printed here, occasionally with slight alterations, are distinguished by his initials (J.E.B.); to him are also due the dates enclosed in square brackets at the head of some of the letters.]

I.

Letters from John Byrom to John Stansfield, 1718—1719.

[Byrom's intimate friend John Stansfield was the recipient of several letters written by Byrom before his marriage, and of one later in date. These are printed in vol. i of *Remains*,, which contains no letter to Stansfield dating from the period covered by the present series. He was a resident in London, where he took part in the management of his father's business. His friendship with Byrom, as the letters in *Remains* show, was based both on personal affection and on community of religious and political opinions, as well as of literary tastes; and Stansfield was useful to his friend in obtaining books and music for him. Byrom, who had been elected a fellow of Trinity in 1714, spent part of the years 1716 and 1717 at Montpelier, where he studied medicine, finally returning to

England in the early part of 1718, and seems to have mainly resided at Cambridge till his marriage in February 1721.

Byrom's fellowship at Trinity, his deep admiration for its great Master, his friendship with the Master's nephew Thomas (Tom) Bentley, 'of our year' (*Remains*, vol. i, p. 25), and his unconcealed regard for Joanna ('Jug'), the Master's second daughter, combined, as a matter of course, to interest him deeply in the long succession of feuds which distracted the University of Cambridge, and Trinity College in particular, during the greater part of Bentley's Mastership. Of these feuds it is impossible to attempt an account here. They are narrated at length in Bishop Monk's *Life of Richard Bentley* (the references to which in the following are to the second edition, revised and corrected, 2 vols., 1833), and admirably summarised in chap. vii of Sir Richard Jebb's *Bentley* (*English Men of Letters*, 1882). One of the acutest stages of the quarrel had been reached in 1718, when, in October, Bentley was deprived of all his academical degrees by a grace of the Senate, while the petition of the Fellows of Trinity, praying the Privy Council to ascertain who was General Visitor of the College (in which wider capacity the Bishop of Ely (Dr. Fleetwood) had declined to act) was still unheard; so that the Master's autocracy still remained unchecked. The petition had been engineered by Sergeant Miller, one of the Fellows of Trinity, and it was he who in February 1717, when it was expected that the Government would appoint a Royal Commission to regulate the affairs of the two Universities, had put forth a long pamphlet,[1] designed at once to direct the

1. *An Account of the University of Cambridge, and the Colleges there. Being a Plain Relation of many of their Oaths, Statutes and Charters. By which will appear, the Necessity the present Members lie under, of endeavouring to obtain such Alterations, as may render them practicable, and more suitable to the present Times. Together with a Few Natural, and Easie Methods, how the Legislature, may for the future fix that, and the other great Nursery of Learning, in the true Interest of the Nation, and Protestant Succession.* Most Humbly propos'd to both Houses of Parliament, By Edmond Miller, Sergeant at Law. London : Printed and sold by J. Baker. 1717.

work of such a commission in a sense contrary to the interests of the High Church Party, and to expose the Master of Trinity and his proceedings to the indignation of a pensive public. Sergeant Miller thus made himself impossible for the future as the agent of Bentley's opponents, and was soon afterwards induced to resign his fellowship for a compensation. The direction of the organised opposition at Trinity was at a later date assumed by Dr. John Colbatch; but, in the meantime, the literary attacks upon Bentley continued. Among these were, besides *A Humble and Serious Representation*,[1] to which Bentley replied by obtaining and publishing a College order denouncing the utmost statutable punishment against any fellow of Trinity convicted of the authorship of the pamphlet, two other pieces certainly written by a former fellow of the College, Conyers Middleton. It was he who sued Bentley in the Vice-Chancellor's court for the repayment of the five guineas exacted from him and other newly-created doctors of divinity by the Regius Professor, on the occasion of the King's visit to the University in October, 1717. These pamphlets, *A Full and Impartial Account*[2] and *A Second Part of the Full and Impartial Account*,[3] were alike Middleton's productions, both of them bearing the date 1719; in the same year he added to them a pamphlet, noticed below, criticising a defence by A. A. Sykes of Bentley's position. It was

1. *A Humble and Serious Representation of the Present State of Trinity College in Cambridge.* In a Letter to a Noble Lord. London : Printed for Bernard Lintot. [December, 1716.] See Richard Bentley, D.D., *A Bibliography of his Works and of all the Literature called forth by his Acts or his writings.* By A. T. Bartholomew, with an Introduction and Chronological Table by J. W. Clark. Cambridge, 1908.

2. *A Full and Impartial Account of all the late Proceedings in the University of Cambridge against Dr. Bentley.* By a Member of the University. London, J. Bettenham, 1719. Price Six Pence.

3. *A Second Part of the Full and Impartial Account of all the late Proceedings in the University of Cambridge against Dr. Bentley.* By a Member of the University. London, J. Bettenham, 1719. Price Six Pence.

against the former two pamphlets—for the third was not published till the reply to its predecessors by the same hand was already in the press[1]—and against the earlier mixed philippic of Sergeant Miller that the pamphlet with which the following letters are concerned was more especially directed. *A Review of the Proceedings against Dr. Bentley,*[2] was published anonymously in 1719; and the secret of its authorship was so well kept by the inner circle to which it was no secret that Bentley's biographer Bishop Monk in 1830 (and again in his second edition, 1833) could speak of the pamphlet as follows, in a passage in which sagacity is curiously mixed with error[3]:

As the pamphlet evidently originated in some degree with Bentley himself, and bore marks of his style, at the same time that it was really unworthy of him, it was conjectured that it might have been drawn up by one of his intimates, and under his own inspection. That it was written by another hand from his dictation, seems highly probable; but the style, the contemptuous tone of criticism, and the peculiar turn of wit, *oblige me to believe the whole of this piece to have proceeded from Bentley.* That its publication, however, was not superintended by him, is found by the extreme carelessness with which it is printed. All his works show him to have been an accurate corrector of the press. In this pamphlet the negligence of the printer seems to respond to the haste and slovenliness with which it was composed. The object was to throw contempt upon the books of Middleton and Miller, and to turn the authors into ridicule. In the case of the Sergeant, who was an awkward and embarrassed writer, the ' Review ' frequently succeeds, and exhibits his strictures in a ludicrous light. Many of the censures are ingenious and humorous, but fall infinitely below what the author of the Remarks on free-thinking was capable of producing; and the whole tone of the book is unfitting a learned, dignified and ill-used divine. It must be allowed, however, that the treatment of Middleton and Miller, contemptuous and insulting as it is, exhibits a less rancorous spirit than may be found in their respective publications against Bentley.

1. Cf. p. 173 and *note* 3, below.
2. *A Review of the Proceedings against Dr. Bentley, in the University of Cambridge : in answer to a late pretended Full and*

It is of course easy enough to be wise after the discovery of the truth; nor could Monk help being unaware of the positive proof afforded by the following letters was not Bentley, but Byrom. The late Sir Richard Jebb, to whom I had the satisfaction of submitting them not long before his lamented death, at once recognised this fact as indisputable. But they further show that, while the pamphlet was written neither by Bentley himself, nor 'by another hand from his dictation,' it cannot be said to have 'evidently originated in some degree with Bentley.' If it bears marks of his style—a question which I am not prepared to decide—this is quite sufficiently accounted for by Byrom's intimate intercourse with the Master, his nephew Thomas (to whom Pope is said to have declared that a well-known couplet in the *Dunciad* was intended to apply, rather than to his great uncle)[1] and his family in general. On the other hand, as these letters show, it is rather hard on Byrom that the carelessness of the printing, which he used his best endeavours to prevent, should be charged against the writer as well as the printer. Curiously enough, if the pamphlet is not altogether in Bentley's manner, neither is it altogether in Byrom's; but he was

1. See *Dict. of Nat. Biogr.*, vol. iv, *s.v.* Bentley, Thomas.

Impartial Account, etc., With some Remarks upon Sergeant Miller's Account of that University; Wherein the Egregious Blunders of that Gentleman are briefly set forth. Solventur risu Tabulæ; Tυ missus abibis. Hor. [*Sat.* bk. ii, *Sat.* i, 1. 86. ' Laughter will quash the case, and you go free.'] ' Ἀνερι ᾿ΑΥΛΗΤΗΡΙ θεοὶ νόον εἰσενέ φυσαν, ᾿Αλλ᾿ ἅμα τῷ φυσᾶν χὠ νύος ἐκπέτατο. ['Into a player on the flute The gods blew sense, the sound to suit; But, as the honest player blew, Both sound and sense from out him flew.'] *Anthol. Epig.* By N.O., M.A. of the same University. London, Printed for E. Moor, near St. Paul's, 1719. Price One Shilling.—As Monk points out, vol. ii, p. 76 note, the title prefixed to the first page of the pamphlet itself differs from that on the title-page proper, being *An Account of Dr. Bentley's Case, in answer to a Pretended Full and Impartial Account, etc.*

3. Monk, vol. ii, pp. 75-6.

young and full of the enthusiasm which makes a good hater
as well as an ardent admirer; and, of all kinds of composition,
controversial prose (more especially in an age addicted to
controversy as few others have been) is least likely to be
successful in the hands of the young and the impetuous.
Moreover, in his attack upon Miller, Byrom had an adversary
whom he detested as a Whig almost as much as he disliked
him as the most active of the Anti-Bentleyites. Yet, as Monk
himself perceived, even so, the writer of the pamphlet kept
within certain bounds—and, herein at least, lovers of Byrom
will recognise that he sought to be true to himself.

It remains to say a word as to the significance of the letters
N.O., under which Byrom, as the writer of the pamphlet,
chose to veil his identity, and of which, in Letter 11, he
promises Stansfield to disclose to him the meaning. One
can hardly suppose that any cryptic ingenuity determined the
choice of these particular letters, similar to that which at a
later date (1721) led Richard Bentley to sign his *Proposals
for printing a New Edition of the Greek Testament J.E.*[1];
still less likely is it that N.O. is inverted for O.N., though
Letter 5 is signed 'Nick.' In Letter 20, Byrom speaks of the
pamphlet as 'a thing Printed for a Sham name by Nobody';
which might seem to favour the idea that N.O. signifies
N . . O=Nemo. But, in Letter 2 of the Letters of Francis
Hooper to John Byrom which follow, *Non Omnino* is given
as the writer's assumption as to the meaning of the title.
This assumption, as being mentioned to Byrom himself, is
not likely to have been erroneous; though for what special
reason he used the phrase (*Non omnino male?*) in the present
connexion, must remain unknown. The passage just quoted
from Letter 20 seems to show that the supposition of Byrom
in Letter 18 was correct, and that the professed printer's
name 'E. Moor, near St. Paul's' was fictitious.]

1. Cf. A. T. Bartholomew, *Bibliography of Richard Bentley* (1908),
No. 78.

I.

Cambridge [Saturday], Decr. 6th, 1718.

Mr. Stansfield,

How do you do? I should be glad to hear from you and should have writ myself to you, but that, to tell you the Truth, I have been a-writing somewhat else, and to who? Why, to our old Friend Mr. Public[1] that writes so many things to us, and about what?—why 'tis about a Business that Mr. Public, an Honest, well meaning man in the main, has been somewhat imposed upon and wants to be set right, they have turned his head with a story about one Dr. Bentley, a great Monster that Havocks Universities, and devours Priveleges as the Dragon of Wantley[2] did Geese and Turkeys &c. Now I have writ a letter to our Friend to inform him of all the particulars concerning this Monster that have happend lately, that Mr. Public may know that the Monster is not so much a Monster as they would make him to be.

1. The same expression occurs in *Remains*, vol. i, p. 65 (J. E. B.), where Byrom is speaking of his *Shorthand Proposals*: ' Now the thing receives a formal publication I shall see what I am likely to expect from my friend Mr. Public, and whether he will have a true relish for clever things or no.' The personification is the Aristophanic Demos translated into the speech of Bunyan.

2. *The Dragon of Wantley* (spelt ' Wanting ' in the MS.). The old ballad of the Dragon of Wantley is to be found in Percy's *Reliques,* ser. iii, bk. iii. The scene of the song, observes the editor, lies about a mile from Wortley, near Rotherham, in Yorkshire, where there "is a Lodge, named Warncliff Lodge, but vulgarly called Wantley. The date of the ballad is said to be early in the seventeenth century, and the writer was clearly inspired by Spenser, though not in the line

' For houses and churches were to him geese and turkies.' "

On this old ballad Henry Carey founded the burlesque opera of *The Dragon of Wantley,* with music by J. F. Lampe, which was produced 26th October 1737, at Covent Garden, and, though temporarily suspended on account of the death of Queen Caroline, had a run of sixty-seven nights. According to Genest, it was performed so late as 1782.

In short, Mr. S., I have prepared a Pamphlet for the Press in answer to that abusive one that came out against Dr. B., and the Business is to get it Printed without being known; not but that it will soon be guessed at from the contents, but that it may not be able to be proved. Mr. Bentley[1] and I were thinking last night that if you would give yourself the trouble of correcting the Press, it might be done with incomparable secrecy, I desire you will not fail to let me know next Post what you say to it, whether you know any Printer of your acquaintance, whether Mr. Pharum[2] would undertake this and be Secret. Anybody will be glad enough on't, for I'm pretty sure 'twill sell well; he will be paid for his work and come in for some share of the Profit that will arise from the Sale &c.

You will let me know by the next Post whether you think it can be done or no, if so, I shall send it you as fast as it can be Printed, it will not take up much time to correct the Sheets as they come from the Press nor be any difficulty to do it for your Eye.

Fail not to write, for we are desirous to have it out now as soon as possible, that it may appear that we have somewhat to say for our Master and our selves, and can give 'em a Rub in their turn. I don't know what you Jacobs[3] think of this Business; but you may depend upon't 'tis nothing but a piece of private enmity covered over with the name of the University; but if you do undertake to get it printed you'll see soon enough whats in't; if you don't care for it, if you think it a Whigg & Tory business &c. or be [so] very Zealous

1. Probably, as p. 159 *et al.* below, Thomas Bentley, the Master's nephew, who in 1718 was a fellow of Trinity, and in that year published his edition of Cicero *De Finibus*.

2. Cf. *Remains*, vol. i, pp. 23, 25 (J. E. B.). In the latter passage Byrom enquires from John Stansfield: ' How does Mr. Pharum do? I have got a good pastoral song by me; if he will have it, he may.' Pharum seems to have been a printer and publisher in London, where Stansfield resided as assistant manager in his father's business.

3. *Jacobs*, Jacobites.

for the Univ. that you won't hear of its Fallibility, let me know,
I wouldn't have you do it except you like it, tho' it would
never be found out this way, when if sent to any of our
University Friends it may.

You will not say a syllable of it to anybody. Our V.C.[1]
will swallow me at a Mouthfull, he has degraded Dr. B[2] &
threatens the Senior Proctor[3] & some others, I shall be
[as] nothing in his Clutches, but if he can't prove the Author I
care not a farthing who knows him. I love Dr. Bentley, they
have used him most unjustly, and I will say my say, I warrant
ye, ffarewell, I expect yours.

If you know not of any Printer &c. we'll let you know of
some or other. Service to Mrs. S. &c.

2.
Cambridge, Decr. 10, 1718.
[Wednesday]

Mr. Stansfield,

To night I have recd yours and Sis: Brearcliffes[4] I am

1. The Vice-Chancellor was Dr. Thomas Gooch, afterwards a
baronet, Master of Caius College, who thrice in succession served the
Office, 1717—1719, and afterwards became Bishop, successively ot
Bristol, Norwich and Ely. Dr. Bentley called him 'the empty
gotch' [a pitcher: the word so occurs in one of Bloomfield's poems]
'of Caius.' (J. E. B.) For a full account of him see Dr. John Venn's
Biographical History of Gonville and Caius College (Cambridge,
1897—1912), vol. i, p. 489, and vol. iii, pp. 115—125.

2. On October 3rd 1718, when Bentley failed to appear before the
Vice-Chancellor's Court, he was declared by the Court to be suspended from all his degrees. A fortnight later (October 16th), a
grace proposing that Bentley's degrees should be not merely suspended but taken away was carried in the Non-Regents' House by
46 votes against 15, and in the Regents' by 62 against 35.

3. In December 1718, the Senior Proctor, who immediately after
the Vice-Chancellor's back was turned, 'took the occasion of a
Speech he was to make to the Scholars, to abuse publicly and grossly
the Conduct and Discipline of the University,' was Dr. [William]
Towers [afterwards, from 1723], Master of Christ's. (Cf. Monk,
vol. ii, p. 76.)

4. Byrom's sister, Sarah, was married, 12 December 1711, to
Thomas Brearcliffe of Halifax. (J. E. B.)

glad that you will see and get my Book printed, which I very willingly commit to your Care, because I know I may depend upon it and your Secrecy concerning it, I here send you as much as will serve to print off half a Sheet on one side, that is, four pages, which I would wish you to get done immediately, and send it me for a Pattern of the letter & Paper which must be clean and handsome, as good, or, better than that in which the Pamphlet which this is in answer to (*A Full and Impartial Acct of the* [late] *Proceedings agnst Dr. B. &c.*) is printed which you may look at and compare it.[1]   The Printer you speak of has the letter &c. and will be careful about it, you may go and propose it to him immediately, you may hear what proposals he makes, and on my part to encourage him, or whoever it be, you may tell he shall be half the Charges and have half the Profit, the book I know will sell very well, and go off great numbers of them, he may however print off a Thousand at first with the Title of first edition, and 500 with the second.[2]

The Price as I guess will be a shilling.[3]   There is no danger from anything said in it but to myself as being an University man, tho' for that Reason you must oblige him to manage so that if possible it may not be known who Printed it, as undoubtedly if he be accustomed to Print Pamphlets he can do, he will to be sure be glad of it and will get money by it, and let him set about it instantly, however, let me know by first what he says to it, whether he is furnished with a good Letter for the Book an Italick, a smaller for quotations & enough for 2 or 3 lines of Greek no more &c. the Book above mentioned will let you see what I mean, otherwise he had better not undertake it, than not make it a Handsome Edition, but if he does, let him get the first half sheet sample done as

1. Cf. for the exact title, *ante*, p. 5, *note*. As a matter of fact, there is not much to choose between the style in which the *Account* and the *Review* are respectively produced.

2. A cunning contrivance (J. E. B.)—but now too common a ' trick of the trade ' to deceive even adolescence.

3. It was actually so priced.

quickly and correctly as can be. You will overlook it and if there be any faults get them amended and so send it to me and if this be done right, the rest you will go on with, and I shall send it you as fast as you want it, you will hear his computation of the Charges &c., in short what he says to it, and tell him he shall come to no loss, but we shall both of us get as much in all appearance as things of this nature yield, and it may be the occasion of further encouragement to him in the Pamphleteering way &c.

Let the sample be of the very same Paper &c. with the whole and ask him how many Sheets he can afford the Public for a Shilling, to get by it.

Decr. 11 [Thursday]. I thought the Carrier had gone out to-day, but he does not till to-morrow when I shall send you as above for half a sheet on one or both sides. Speak to the man and let me hear from you every Post, be sure let not my name be named in it to anybody, I would have you buy the Pamphlet above and give me your thoughts on't, ask the man how soon he can publish this abroad &c. and take care it be not a Scrub letter or Paper, if you read the Book against Dr. B. you'll not wonder so much if I should make a little free with his Enemies, what we see our Hero abused suffer wrong and not say a word for him or ourselves? no no.

I Have been busy preparing for you and have not time to answer Sis: Brearcliffes Letter about the Library keepers Place.[1] Mr. Davenport[2] has writ to Mr. Hooper[3] about it who I believe will put in for't tho' I really think he had better not, for it will prejudice him in Relation to Fellowships

1. The Librarianship of Chetham's Library, Manchester, vacant by the death of Jas. Leicester. Cf. *Remains*, vol. i, p 41 (J. E. B.), as to Byrom's willingness to ' have the Library '; and see below, pp. 181 and *introductory note*

2. No doubt the F. Da . . t mentioned in *Remains*, vol. i, p. 29 note (Davenport, *ib.*, p. 266). Cf. *ante*, p. 4, *An Invitation to Breakfast, note.*

3. As to the Rev. Francis Hooper see below, p. 179 (*introductory note*).

which he would make a bad bargain to risk for the Other. You may tell my Brother[1] that if Oaths or Orders are not necessary, as I conceive they are not and he thinks fit I should put in for it, with all my Heart. Mr. D. tells Mr. Hooper of Punctilio's, Qualifications, truth[2] to the Gov: &c. that neither he nor I know what he means.

My dear Love to 'em all & tell 'em I long to have my abode with them as much as they do. Mr. Bentley presents his service. We expect Massey[3] here shortly. My Hearty service to Mrs. Stansfield. How does my Daughter[4] do? *Allons! Courage! Adieu*—O! Regent [!] Cellamare![5]

3.

Cambridge [Sunday], Decr. 14, 1718.

Mr. Stansfield,

I sent you on Friday part of my Book which you have or will get printed off as soon as possible, there was an omission which I forgot to supply: 'tis in these words " that were forc't to pay a Matter of (20lb) for a Degree which at another time wouldn't have cost 'em above a (100) and insert after

1. Edward Byrom (J. E. B.).
2. *Truth.* If this is a misprint for 'Oath' it can hardly refer to the then still unrepealed clause of the Corporation Act, requiring all persons bearing offices of trust in corporations to swear that resistance in arms to the King was unlawful; while no private test is likely to have been imposed by the authorities of the Chetham Hospital or Library.
3. No doubt Byrom's friend Massey, frequently mentioned in *Remains* (vol. i, p. 57 *et al.*).
4. My daughter. Cf. below, p. 27. Probably Mrs. Stansfield.
5. This exclamation seems to read in the MS.: *O! Regent Cellamare.* But, inasmuch as it was because of his taking the leading part in the conspiracy against the Regent Orléans in 1718 that the Prince of Cellamare (Duke of Giovenazza), when Spanish ambassador at Paris, was arrested there by order of Cardinal Dubois and transported across the frontier, I have ventured on the above conjecture. Cellamare's case caused a great sensation, and figures among the *Causes célèbres du droit des gens* in C. von Martens' collection.

these words 'who took some of 'em not 4 but, (very near)
14 Guineas.'[1]"   I depend upon your care in getting this done
handsomely, and without all Question somewhat may be got
by it, tho' I must own myself more concerned for the Cause
than the Profit.   However, that need not be neglected, I
suppose the man is used to print such things, and knows the
way of getting 'em off, he may sell 2 or 300 of 'em here, a 100
pages abt which is a Pamphlet for 12d may be printed for a
groat with any tolerable Quantity, you need not be cautious
as to the Printer, for none can hurt you, but me only.   I writ
this Post to my Brother about the library, Mr. Hooper and I
have agreed to manage it together if the people that govern
this affair are wise enough to agree to it.   We are going to
Chapel, I just come from drinking Tea with our Mistress [2];
she tells us the Schism Bill[3] is going to be repealed, which
may perhaps be news to you, nothing being said of it as I
saw in the Papers.   They talk of 2 Visitations, one for our
Univ. another for our Coll : we shall see in Time.   The late
Lib. Keeper[4] we hear is resolv'd to write a Pamphlet against
our V.C. whose treatment of him he complains of mightily,

1. This last addition was not inserted. The reference of course
is to the action begun by Dr. Conyers Middleton against Vice-
Chancellor Bentley in the V.C. Court in 1718 to try the right of the
latter to a fee of four guineas which Bentley claimed for Middleton's
degree of D.D. conferred on George I's visit to the University in 1717.
(J. E. B.) For the whole business see Monk, vol. ii, pp. 37 *sqq.*;
and cf. Jebb, pp. 114-5.

2. Mrs. Bentley (Johanna Bernard), who 'managed everything'
in Trinity Lodge, besides going through her daily task of 'trying,
like Mrs. Thrale, to be civil for two.' (Jebb).

3. 'The Schism Act, which restricted the education of the
Dissenters, and the Occasional Conformity Act, which was intended
to restrict their political power, were both repealed in 1718.' (Lecky,
History of England in the Eighteenth Century, vol. i, p. 258, where
see more on the subject.)

4. Philip Brooke, B.D., Fellow of St. John's College and University Librarian. Proceedings were taken against him in the Vice-
Chancellor's Court for disaffection to the King; but on his resignation
of his office the action was stayed (J. E. B.).

having made him believe that he was his sure friend & now shewn the contrary. If it be not set you may order rather a less Character than that of the Pamphlet I told you of, for I shall find it more difficult to reduce my business within an 100 Pages than to exceed.

Let me hear from you. My service to all friends Mrs. S. especially. Mr. Bent. gives service & is glad you undertake this, his Concern is lest the man shouldn't do it neatly &c. I will send you more when you want.

Yrs.

4.

Sunday just 6 o'clock.
[21 December].

Mr. Stansfield,

I this moment rec^d yours, if the Post wont go out before I have done I can tell you I have seen and read the Pamphlets you mention, which will not hinder me at all from going on, tho' perhaps they may occasion some little variation in my Copy which it is no matter if it stays so long now since it will look as an Answer to both these Pamphlets against the Dr. I will send you 5lbs and you'll send me the half sheet, and write by the Post by whom; never fear the sale of this Business, here have been more than 200 sold here by the others. I am sorry for Jemmy [1] & hope with you his eyes will grow well again.

Yrs.

5.

Monday, Decr. 15, 1718.

Mr. S.,

I Rec^d yours last night, I write here by the Carrier that I may have your answer on Wednesday, I hope you have got the sample printed off if not, let it be done out of Hand, if the Printer scruples to do anything in't let it be done on my own Charges, so much more will be got by it for I know

1. As to Byrom's interest in Stansfield's children, cf. *Remains*, vol. i, pp. 41-2, and see his letter, justly termed 'beautiful and manly' by Canon Parkinson, on the death of one of them (the eldest), *ib.*, p. 26.

something will. However, to encrease his Case when I tell him I will secure him from loss and there is such a probability of Gain, I have no notion of his refusing it. I will send you Money when you please but I must wait for the Opportunity of a Bill or some other way not daring to send it by the Carrier for fear of Suspicion.

No offence to yr Printer, if as good Judgements as his are past upon the Success of this Pamphlet, I cannot so conveniently send it together as by pieces, new circumstances arise every day amongst us proper to be noticed, I know not what I can say more that the Business may go on, I suppose as you say, it will be done well if the Printer of the St. J. Post[1] does it. You will not fail to let me know how you go on, & to send me the Pattern whereby to guess how much will serve for the Book &c.

Mr. Hooper is this Minute gone down to Lancashire about the Lib:[2] which he and I have agreed to assist each other in, whoever is Chosen. We have 3 of our Coll: put in for our Lib: Keepers place[3] & 2 or 3 more, I am in hopes one of Mr. Bs intimates and mine who knows well of the Pamphlet will get it. My Blessing to my Daughter and Grandchild.[4] I fear being too Late for the Carrier

Ffarewell & be Chearfull
Yrs.

Mrs. S. How do you do?
I have a piece of potted Ven :
just sent me from a Lanc.
Lad, will you eat a little
with me.

Nick.[5] Amen.

1. St. James' Post (J. E. B.).

2. The Chetham Library.

3. Cf. *ante*, p. 23 and note. The University Librarian actually elected was Thomas Macro, M.A. (afterwards D.D.), of Gonville and Caius College, a Bury St. Edmunds man, who held the office from 1718 to 1721. He published some sermons. He was the brother of the antiquary Cox Macro. See Venn, *u.s.*, vol. i, p. 506.

4. These names were, perhaps, given by Byrom to Stansfield's wife and child. See above, p. 21.

5. Probably a *nickname*. As to the significance of ' N.O.' on the title-page see *introductory note, ante*.

6.

Sunday Night [21 December 1718, J.E.B.].

Mr. Stansfield,

I have expected to hear from you and to receive the half sheet this week. I should be glad if you would give yourself the trouble of writing a line of a Post-night, pray do, and if you would either send or Copy out the rest of what I sent you which is not Printed I shall thank you, because this Second Part of the Book against Dr. B.[1] may give occasion for some variation, the Latin you need not copy, I beg that I may hear from you. I Have desired Mr. Bentley who will get a Bill from Crownfield our Printer[2] for 5lbs which I shall send you. Don't your Printer work in the Holidays? I Rec^d a Letter from my Brother this week wherein he is angry at what I have done about the Library Keepers Place at Manchester, tho' I profess by Sis. Brearcliffes Letter I imagined it to be their Inclination that I should do somewhat ab^t it, or I should not have troubled my head with it, Mr. H.[3] he intimates is not likely to get it.

Pray wish all Friends a Merry Happy Xmas for me, and enjoy the same yourselves as wishes

Yrs.

Green Dragon.

7.

Mr. Stansfield,

I went to the Carriers, expecting to meet with what you said you had to send, but I saw the Carrier himself, the same man that I came with from London and he looked over his Papers & said there was nothing for me. I write to know

1. *A Second Part of the Full and Impartial Account.* (See above.)
2. Cornelius Crownfield, University Printer, 1705—1740.
3. Hooper.

L

whether you carried it to the Green Dragon[1] or to some other Inn there, or how it is that I received 'em not. I do not question but we shall find it better corrected than what I did myself, which has a world of Faults, and that is the reason I was desirous of a 2d Edition, and to have some fewer in the first if it could have been. I tho't you had told me once that he would keep his letters Set. I shall order 200 hither, but when will it be out at the Rate it goes on? His delays are *fort mal a propos* as John Frenchman says, at a Juncture when half a Dozen accidents may render the Book less Proper, which if would but out, would be of Use.

When you told my Bro. of it you would caution him against mentioning it to any Body, if Mr. Hooper or &c. should know it would be no secret here soon. I think if you send my Bro. one or 2 and he shews it W. C.[2] and he has a mind to send for any he may but pray let him (Bro.) know that if it be known proveably that 'tis mine they'll eat me up as a Man would eat an Apple John.[3] If I have time (for 'tis a busy Day with me, I have been before the Seniors about getting a Chamber[4] this morn) I'le write to him myself, Tom B's Calculation of 4lb he says is not exact but he thinks the Paper Dear: but the Business is to get it out, it should have been done by his own Computation, pray hasten him and please [be] particular to let me know next Post whether he cannot have room for another Page in 5 Sheets & a ½ or if he wants more to fill up, and be sure let him not lessen the

1. *The Green Dragon* in Bishopsgate Street was one of the inns from which the Cambridge coach regularly started. (See C. G. Harper, *The Cambridge, Ely and King's Lynn Road* (1892), pp. 8, 12 *et al.*)

2. W.C.; no doubt, as Mr. Sutton has suggested to me, William Clayton, bookseller in Manchester, father of the Rev. John Clayton (cf. *introductory note*, pp. 110 *sq., ante*).

3. An apple ripened late in the season and considered good when shrivelled. See Shakspere, *Henry IV*, Part I, act III, sc. 3, l. 4, and Part ii, act ii, sc. 4, l. 2. (J. E. B.)

4. Rooms in College.

Character whatever happens, please to alter, if it ben't printed, in the latter End about Trinity Coll :[1]

> That Ten Dividends are not more than Twenty, or that two or three and Twenty Lads a Year admitted in Dr. M-gues[2] Time, are not more than Forty in Dr. Bentleys.—

So let it be,[3] for tho' some Years had extremely few yet I have pitch't upon a more moderate Comput- I earnestly entreat to hear from you, you'll send it as fast as workt off more or less by post or Carrier any day. I look for the Title to-morrow night and you shall have it again as soon as Poss.

Mr. Bentley gives service to Mrs. S. and wishes the little Toper his Legs, I told him the story and he laughed most intolerably.

Yrs.

8.

[Sunday] Jany. 4, 1719.

Mr. Stansfield,

I send you herein enclosed a Bill of Five Pounds which you may receive when you call for it. I cant concieve what your Printer sticks at, cannot he do what I order him, you say he does not understand my meaning but you don't tell me as to what. I have expected his Sample a long while, pray be so kind as to write next Post &c. you may send it by the Carrier from Bishopsgate Street any day or the Coach &c. The man shall lose nothing by any alterations that shall be made, I shall complete my Copy as soon as I can but would willingly see this sample first. I do not know whether I shall hear from you to-night or no if not pray return my services to Mrs. S. &c. and I return you all yr wishes of a Happy New Year and full of good events,

I am Yrs.

1. Apparently the passage meant is that on p. 71, which records the fact that only four Fellows of Trinity could be brought to vote for the degradation of their Master.

2. Dr. John Montagu (afterwards Dean of Durham) was Master of Trinity from 1683 to 1700, when he was succeeded by Bentley.

3. The passage stands thus in the printed pamphlet.

9.

Cambridge, Jan. 8th [thursday], 1719.

Mr. Stansfield,

I have rec^d the Sample Last Post, which falls much short of what I desired it should come up to viz : that it should be full good as the Pamphlet I wrote against, which I here send you a piece of since you may not perhaps have bought it, and you will see the Difference. I easily presume the Printer of the St. James's Post has a better and a fairer letter & the Paper is soon changed. I have said often enough he shall be no loser by it and I hope to hear from you in answer to this that he will mend his hand upon't. I could wish you to compare the Pamphlet and you'll judge of the fitness of a better Character.

Mr. Bentley returns his Services to you with the wishes of a Happy New Year &c. and wishes the Man mav do this Pamphlet in a better Character and Paper, you will let us know by next whether he can or no. He shall be paid for this first Attempt, but he must make use of better, fresher, Letters &c. I Congratulate you upon your Membership of the Quest,[1] but pray what do you Quest men do? What is your Office? I desire to hear from you next Post, and am with service to Mrs. S. &c.

Yrs.

Pray Favour me with a line next Post, this is an old weatherbeaten Character & but bad Ink, 'tis enough to make nobody read it, I would have it well done cost what it will, 'tis well corrected, there are not many errata's in it.

10.

Trin : Coll : [Sunday] Jan. 18, 1719.

Mr. Stansfield,

I thank you for Yours and your Promise to take care that the Letter & Paper shall please, I here send you the Sample

1. *The Quest.* Possibly a board of enquiry or inquest connected with a city of London company.

which I should have sent in my last but forgot it, and will get ready the whole of my Copy as fast as I can. I Have recd a Letter from Mr. Hooper who hopes to be chosen, the Election is on the 22d of this Month. We have chose Mr. Thirlby of Jesus[1] (that writ in defence of Athanasius against Whiston) deputy Registrar to supply the Place of Mr. Grove of St. Johns[2] the Registrar who run Mad just after Dr. Bentleys business but is we hear in a hopeful way of recovery at London, the V. Chancellor had promised two parties and acted very oddly with both, proposed a Grace himself in the morning & Voted against it in the afternoon the Reflection made on his Conduct is that 'tis the way to bring in Dr. B. with the University's good liking. Have you heard of the Presbyterian Synod at Exeter where the famous Peirce & 16 more declared openly for Arianism & this was the occasion of the rejected Clause about the Trinity &c.[3] My Service to Mrs. S. Yrs.

1. Styan Thirlby, B.A. 1704, M.A. 1720, LL.D., editor of Justin Martyr's Works (J. E. B.). For an account of him see *Dictionary of Biography,* vol. lvi, where he is stated to have published, anonymously, in 1710, a pamphlet, *The University of Cambridge vindicated from the Imputation of Disloyalty it lies under on account of not addressing* [the King]; *is also from the malicious and foul Aspersions of Dr. Bentley, late Master of Trinity College, etc.* Byrom may not have been aware of Thirlby's authorship of this pamphlet. An *Answer to Mr. Whiston's Seventeen Suspicions concerning Athanasius, in his Historical Preface* appeared in Cambridge in 1712 and was followed by other tracts on the subject.

2. Robert Grove, St. John's College, B.A. 1691; M.A. 1695; Public Registrar 1701. *Graduate Cantabrigienses* (1823), p. 204. He held the office till 1726, when Lancelot Newton, M.A. (afterwards LL.D.), of St. John's, was elected his successor.

3. See J. Murch, *History of the Presbyterian and General Baptist Churches in the West of England* (1835), and E. Calamy, *Life and Times,* vol. ii (J. E. B.). Calamy narrates (pp. 403 *sqq.*) how the differences among the Nonconformists at Exeter as to the doctrine of the Trinity existed by the teaching of James Peirce, minister at the St. James' Meeting, Exeter, from 1713 to 1729, were brought into the

11.

Mr. S.,

You will receive this on Thursday noon [22nd December] pray carry it immediately to the Printers, and let him get it done to send a Sample in a Post Letter at Night because a Fault in the Title Page should not be, and Let it be as handsome as he can make it. By N.O. M.A. of the S[ame] U. must be all in a line. I shall tell you after why we have called the Author N.O.[1]

I have just time to send this by the Carrier, they are at Dinner in the Hall, eating Oisters. I beg of you to let me have it on Friday. ffarewell good now[2] hasten the Man all you can,

Yrs.

If you have not printed in the Acc^t of Trin : College these words *because Trinity College is the handsomest in Europe* alter it to because *Trinity College* is one of the handsomest in *Europe.*[3] I cant think if I have anything else to say. Oh! tell the Printer he must not advertize it till he has sent some Books hither as I shall order to-morrow.

12.

Mr. S.,

I sent to you by Thursdays Coach that I might hear from you on Friday, but I find it has miscarried for I have none

1. See Preface.

2. *Good now.* Cf. *Hamlet,* act i, sc. 1 : 'Good now, sit down and tell me.'

3. The alteration—a very remarkable one for a Trinity man to suggest—was actually made.

Assembly of Ministers which met there in September 1718. Although a Trinitarian resolution was passed by the Assembly, an active controversy ensued, and the Exeter Nonconformists were advised by a narrow majority in a meeting held at Salters Hall, London, in 1719, to abstain from a particular declaration of their faith in the Holy Trinity. Peirce, with two other Exeter ministers was, however, ejected. Murch also gives a long account of the controversy (pp. 386—401), with a notice of Peirce (pp. 421-31).

from you neither last Post nor this, which has deprived me of a very great satisfaction, I question not but I may seem more concerned about my Book than you may think the Book worth but as it is the Strictest rule of our Profession[1] to end an Adventure well you must excuse me for my K^t Errantry in this. My Wise Publisher has astonished not myself only but all our People here by the particular Management of sending a Dozen of 'em when the whole Impression of 'em would have been sold off in an Instant, last night Webster [of] whom I ordered only 50 told Mr. Walker and I that if he had 500 he could have sold 'em, that he was plagued out of his Life for 'em & and 'tis the same with the Rest of 'em. In short 'tis quite wrong in 'em and if there can be any persuading 'em to be less ill Managers I should be glad, the Book is lik't, Dr. Bently is well pleased and all our Friends and our Enemies may guern[2] as they please it is fixt upon me all Town over but there being no Proof all is well, it strikes 6 and I have but just Time if that to present my Dr love to my Sis: &c. and to desire once more for — sake that you'll let me hear from you,

　　　　　ffarewell.
good now, lets have some more, there must be a 2d E.

13.

　　　　　　　　　Thursday, Feby. 19.
S.,
　We had a very good Journey, and gott hither before Dinner to-day. You will believe what a merry sort of a Welcome I met with, here was a Fellow Commoner went to accompany his Brother 10 Miles and stayed out 10 Days, but it can be proved upon [him] that he took 2 shirts so that he cannot come near me. No Soul guesses what I have been about. Mr. Bent. and Walker think it Long, you must hasten the man all thats Possible, the Corrections I think

1. The Medical, I suppose, in which it is not etiquette to hand over a case.
2. *Guern* (girn), snarl.

you'll do, but when you scruple let me know, the last Greek
verse must be thus[1]:

You see that word under the Cross must be alter'd I shall
send you the Title Page &c. next Post. I have scarce Time
now to present my Service to you & Mrs. S. and to wish little
Toper the continuance of his Health, having been this Afternoon in Co with Friends, tell Coz Chad.[2] that Cos. Dicky
Allen[3] is coming up to Coll : the beginning of next Month.

they laugh at my Correcting, we must make Erratas &c.[4]

ffarewell.

[Postscript, from Thomas Bentley.]

Mr. Stansfield, all Mr. Byrom's friends here are very angry
that Warner[5] is so slow; what! only 3 half sheets in 3 weeks,
he might have printed ten folio's in the time. pray, lets have
it in ten days at least.

I am glad to hear your little Boy is recovered. My humble
Service to Mrs. Stansfield,

& to yourself, from Your

obliged friend   T. Bentley.

14.

Trin : Coll : [Saturday] Feb. 21, 1719.

Mr. Stansfield,

How do you do? how does friend Warner go on? We

1. See p. 33 of the original pamphlet.
2. *Coz. Chad.* As to Byrom's ' cousin Chaddocks ' see *Remains*,
vol. i, p. 61. A letter from Mr. Chaddock, one of Byrom's lifelong
friends, appears *ib.*, vol. ii, p. 288.
3. *Cos. Dicky Allen.* Probably Richard Allen of Reddivales, who
seems to be the ' cos. Dicken ' of *Remains*, vol. ii, p. 433. I can find
no Richard Allen of this period in the *Graduati.*
4. There is a fairly large list of *errata* at the end of the pamphlet.
One of these corrects the epithet *insolvent* as applied to Bentley by
his assailant, into *insolent.*
5. This seems to have been the London printer's name

are in Expectation here of something by way of Pamphlet from our Adversaries and are very desirous your Recruit may arrive before the Enemy gets more forces into Melazzo.[1]

Pray be so kind as to send without Fail by Wednesdays Carrier what is set more or less, and you may keep going on.

Bentley and Walker question the Mans dealing cleverly, they say he might afford more than 5 sheets and [a] half but that you must tell him he must have, and if he will have another half sheet he may, he can judge by this time how it goes towards filling. I would insert a Par. if he has room, 4lb they say is as much as 'twill cost him in all but perhaps it wont however pray ask him how many Copies he prints I suppose 500.

I think you told me the Letters would remain set for a 2d Edition if occasion which I believe there will be, and then we can correct the many Blunders in Typography which I have overlookt in this first, of which Walker has remarked only about 30.

You must be very urgent with him to dispatch, and see that he does not be negligent or imposing and learn what number he works off and let him think of a Second Edition.

Tom. Bently will be here with me by and by, if we agree on the Title shall send it for next Post. There is one Favour I must desire of you about the Grace[2] concerning Dr. Bently (we cannot get it here) that you'll step to the Printer of the Post Boy or Evening Post I think it was in both but Post Boy I am sure, and get the Copy of it if you can't meet with it in the Coffee-Houses, I have none from you this Post, but shall be glad to have next, Little Toper I hope is better and better every Day; do you hear yet when my Sister is for coming

1. In the early part of 1719, great interest was taken in the siege of Melazzo in Sicily, carried on by the Spaniards after the reduction of Messina ; and the siege was not raised by the Imperialists till May.

2. The grace for degrading him, which is printed at length *ap.* Monk, vol. ii, pp. 58-9.

up. · Dr. Andrew has lost his Cause against Beadle Clarke[1] about the Groats didn't I tell you about it. The V.C. [Dr. Gooch] was bail for the Beadle which was thot to be somewhat extraordinary, that the Judge should be Bail.　ffarewell.
How do you do Madam.　　　　　　　　　Yours　T. B.[2]

15.
Trin : Coll : St. Mathias [24 Feby] 1719.
Mr. Stansfield,

I told you I would send you the Title this Post, Walker and Bentley have been drinking tea with me this afternoon and we have not fixed on't, but shall in my next.

They are very solicitous for its coming out soon, are afraid that somebody that should not may see it at the Printers all this while, that another business on the other side should get out before it, besides a Determination[3] which we still look for every day would spoil the timing of it, and are very urgent with me to get the man to get it out immediately. I think he promised you it should be done this week, and will I hope take care accordingly, they do not question its doing good service, and selling enough, I shall tell the Printer if he will what Bookseller to send a number to here at Camb :

Please to alter in the last Page or two[4] about the Register "tho for any Power that he had of tendering him his Oath in that Manner he might &c." let it be thus printed instead of tendring an Oath in General as I think it is in the copy. again—This Consenting and not Consenting ends, as Dr. M. says, in desiring & let it be thus. I would send you the

1. Edward Clarke, Esquire Bedell. He had been charged to arrest Dr. Bentley, September 1718, when the Doctor locked him up in his Lodge for several hours (J. E. B.). Cf. Monk, vol. ii, p. 50. I do not know what was the cause of Dr. Andrew (John Andrew, LL.D. of Trinity Hall ?) against the Esquire Bedell.

2. This line was evidently added by Thomas Bentley.

3. The ' Determination ' in question must be the Royal Commission which it was thought likely would be appointed after the Degradation proceedings had been laid by the Vice-Chancellor before the King in Council. (See Monk, vol. ii, pp. 64-5.)

4. *A Review, etc.,* p. 78. The passage was altered accordingly.

Paragraph I would have inserted but have not Time and shall wait to hear how you go on to-morrow.

Massey is going to be married to the Daughter at the Popes Head,[1] they say he will not have his Christ Hospital Living because he refuses to reside. How does Jemmy yet? do you know that a namesake of his is going to be married to the Infanta of Spain?[2] that there is to be an Interview between him and K.G. let me know if there is any talk of my Country Folks coming up or no. I Have writ to Aunt Allen, Clowes, Cos. Ann. Byrom and Mr. Hooper, whom I had letters from in my Absence only the last.

We were last night to hear the Famous Harper, Morphy,[3]

1. I cannot explain this passage. Mr. Massey (who is frequently mentioned by Byrom in the *Remains*, where he is sometimes called Dr. Massey) seems to have frequented the Pope's Head (probably the tavern so called in Cornhill, which gives its name to Pope's Head Alley; but there were other Pope's Head Taverns in Chancery Lane, in Dowgate, and in Lombard Street) where some kind of club was held in the winter (*Remains*, vol. i, p. 156). Soon afterwards Byrom met him in the Court of Requests, where he probably practised as a barrister (*ib.*, p. 193). His lady is mentioned as walking with him in the Park (ib., p. 204).

2. Jemmy (Stansfield's) namesake was of course the Old Pretender, whose marriage to Princess Clementine Sobiesky did not take place till September 1719. The interview wtih ' K.G.,' like the marriage with the Infanta, failed to ' come off.' For the relatives mentioned below see *Remains*. Aunt Allen is Mrs. Allen, cf. *Remains*, vol. i, p. 370; Clowes, Joseph Clowes, Esq., who frequently figures in the *Remains*; Coz. Ann Byrom, a daughter of Byrom's uncle, Joseph Byrom (cf. *Remains*, vol. i, p. 43 *et al.*).

3. *The Famous Harper, Morphy.* I owe to Mr. Sutton the following extract from W. H. G. Flood, *History of Irish Music* (Dublin, 1905) : ' Perhaps the most popular of O'Carolan's contemporaries, after Cornelius Lyons, was John Murphy of County Wexford . . . (who) performed before Louis XIV about the year 1710. In one of the Dublin papers of the year 1737-8 I find a notice that on February 4th, 1738, John Murphy, the Irish harper, was one of the attractions at Smock-alley Theatre, when a double bill was presented in aid of the poor prisoners in the city Marshalsea . . . . The last I find of Murphy is his appearance at the various assemblies held at Mallow between the years 1746 and 1753 . . .'

it was the first time I heard him, 'tis a glorious Instrument, we had ladies there, Mrs. Vice-Chancellor was there under the conduct of Dr. Middleton, whose wife one of the Beadles handed, but Jug![1] was not there Heigh! Ho! ffare ye well Ile go take an Hatchet and hang myself,[2] farewell Mrs. Stansfield.

Mr. Bentley and Walker give their Services, Mr. Walker says this Mr. Stansfield of yours is a very clever fellow, but I doubt the Printer is so diligent as he might be; his Mans Sore eyes he thinks are not got with Poring o'er my business.

16.

Trin : Coll : March 8, 1719.

Mr. Stansfield,

Mr. Walker and I are just this moment 4 o'clock returned from Huntington whither we have brought out friend Mr. Bentley on his way to Yorkshire who sends his service to honest Mr. S. and his wife.

I received the Sheets on Saturday and here send you the Erratas which must be inserted in the empty Page on the other side of the Title.

Give this under to the Printer

[*a piece is here cut out of the MS.*]

There are many more Errata's but these must be taken notice of on for the Title and 2 Pages that are not worked off, you will see that they be corrected thus

At p. 81 the Page itself is printed 18 instead of 81. line 5 Principal instead of Principle. line 6 Complainsance for Complaisance. line 15 Preforment for Preferment, and line 27 several words of the Copy are left out, so as if this had been worked off it must have been done again.

I would not be guilty of Indifference to Merit (not Indifferent to merit, as it is printed) which must be corrected,

1. '*Jug.*' Joanna Bentley. See *ante*, vol. i, p. 3, *note*.
2. Jack Cade tells Lord Say, when he speaks of himself as sick (*Henry VI*, Part II, act iv, sc. 7, ll. 80-1) : ' Ye shall have a hempen caudle then and the help of hatchet.'

rence, and great M) nor of Unconcernedness at its . . . .
Magistrates; pray see it right thus & in your copy I suppose
nor of Unconcernedness at its oppression; I love the University, and I honour its Magistrates, 'tis well this omission is
not worked off, it would have made irrecoverable nonsence of
the sentence, then P. 82.   13 another must be one word.
8 Deternation. Determination. 12 preceived. perceived.
13 Bentley, with a Comma and the next word Congratulat
a little c and no e at the end.[1]   We beg of you to desire Mr.
G.[2] to deliver his Books and cause them to be sent by the
Coach which comes out on Wednesday morning and so they
will be here before the Judge Dr. B. Sergeant Miller &c.
are gone which otherwise they will not.

17.

T. C., March 5, 1719.

Mr. Stansfield,
   I was not without hopes of receiving all from you to-day
and alas!   I have received nothing, pray, pray, this Idle
fellow is vexatious, didn't he say Wednesday all would be
proved off? here we have a third Part of Middletons Book
come out,[3] I believe you knew on't; sure if you will but make
hast this 3d Part is the best Introduction for the Pamphlet
that can be as it happens. Good now, buy it and see how
he bullies in his fourpeny Business upon Dr. Bs friends
inability to answer him. &c.   I wait with the utmost Impati-
ence to have this Contrivance once out and then let it take its
Fortune, surely he has set all the last Sheet.   I must see
before 'tis worked off that I may gather the Erratas out of
the whole Book, for whose Insertion he must Leave Room

   1. The printer retained the capital C and the e at the end. The
other changes he seems to have made.
   2. Mr. G. may have been the publisher or stationer.
   3. This is *Some Remarks upon a Pamphlet* [by A. A. Sykes, of
Corpus Christi College, M.A. 1708, D.D. 1726] *entitled, The Case of
Dr. Bentley Further Stated and Vindicated, etc.* By the author of the
Full and Impartial Account, etc. (Price Four Pence.)

and an Advert. of a few Lines. I doubted not of 2 Sheets at least to-day, Tuesday I wrote not.

Mr. Bentley & I rode to meet the Dr. who is come to Coll. for a few days. I have a rare Adventure here upon my Hands about an House.[1] We are mounted on the High Horse of Dispute & the Victory, if Malicious Enchanters who I believe obstruct our Printers Printing do not prevent it, will fall to your Valorous Humble Servt and Mrs. Stans.,

T. B.[2]

Mr. Stansfield, Our Friend Mr. Bentley received a letter last night at Supper with the melancholy news of his Fathers sudden Death in Yorkshire, I have been Ministering all the Comfort I can to him and he is pretty Cheerful, I carried the news from him to the Dr. last night who is now the only one left of 4 or 5 that have died, the youngest first. One, a Sister, but 3 weeks before her Brother, Tom[s] Father,[3] he succeeds to a very plentiful Estate, which he is going down to look at.

18.

Mr. S.,

I thank you for the Book which I read last night. Mr. Walker and I were lamenting that nothing was come that Day till the Man brought this to alleviate our grief. By Monday Coach I suppose we may expect some to be sent to the Booksellers, as I mentioned formerly, Crownfield 100, Webster 50, Jeffries 500, or, as they shall otherwise Correspond [?] it. If they do not come on Monday let me entreat you to procure 'em to be sent on Monday night for the Coach

1. *Query,* Horse?

2. I do not understand these initials, as ' Tom ' Bentley is mentioned in the text.

3. Thomas Bentley, was the son of James Bentley, the eldest son of Thomas Bentley of Woodlesford, and elder brother of the great Richard Bentley. The small estate was at Woodlesford, one of the five townships of which the parish of Rothwell, near Wakefield, consists. (Monk, vol. i, pp. 1-2.)

on Tuesday if so many ben't stitcht, tho' I suppose all may by that time let those be sent that are, for on Wednesday morning a Yorkshire Carrier goes out by whom we shall send some to some friends in those parts, which opportunity we would not lose. We are very glad that you have managed to have 'em out at last and think nothing will be known of it, since Mr. G. and W. carry it so privately. I see they Printed the Erratas off before my three last came to your hand to be inserted. This E. Moor is a feigned name is it not?[1] It is a favourable aspect of the Stars if the Books come in Mondays Coach, for they cannot fail of success coming under Jugs auspices whom I told you we expected on Friday, but, to-morrow certain. I shall mount my Steed and go in Quest of her and conduct her to the Knight her Father's Castle, as will Mr. Walker. I am got into Tom: Bentleys house and want to hear of Cousin Allens coming up that I may keep M. Hooper for him till I can get him a Chr[2] of his own.

I Hope no harm is come to any of our friends a travelling you will see 'em I hope by this arrives at you, & pray my dear love to Sis: Betty,[3] and hearty service to 'em all. Fail not I pray to write me word whether they are with you or No, and how they all do &c.

The strange Appearance in the Air[4] was seen here just as you describe, and portends wonderful things but what they be
   Time will discover perhaps—

Farewell.

Secure us some Books in Tuesday Coach.

19.

Mr. S.,

How do you do? I should have been glad to have heard from you these last Posts and am somewhat in Pain that I have not, there have come 12 to Crownfield then 25 then 50

1. Such seems to have been the case. Cf. *Letter* 20 below.
2. *Chamber.* Rooms in College.
3. Elizabeth Byrom.
4. The strange appearance in the air may have been a not strictly meteorological phenomenon.

to Webster of the Books which he sold off instantly. I know not to what to attribute the sending 'em here in this Manner, if they had studied to spoil the Sale of it, they could not have done it more effectually, nor a done more prejudice to the Book, here was a Report that the Author and his Friends had bo'tt up the Impression because there were so many False Facts in it; that there was a letter forged upon the V.C. which he had never wrote &c. and a world of wrong Notions for want of the Books being seen. Dr. Bentley says there is not a single fact but what is true, if there be, let'em shew it us and welcome, Walker had a letter from one of our Noblemen at Lond. of Xt Coll:[1] a great Enemy to our cause who enquires of him abt the Ingenious Review as he calls it, and they are stupid Owls that dont see that 'tis writ exceeding cleverly, I like it myself upon 2 reading of it entire. Dr. Baker[2] thankt me for it t'other Day, Me Sir say I? well says he I don't know who 'tis, but we are very much obliged to him; there is no Question amongst us of its being mine, but 'tis only Suspicion. I long to hear from you if you have any news of it at London, Let me hear however tho' I almost despair thro' your Silence at present.

Mr. Bently sends his Service to you out of Yorkshire, is very eager for News about the Book, I could not get one to send him till to-day. Pray my Service &c. to Mrs. Stans: & give me the pleasure to hear how you all do, ffarewell.

Yrs with all Possible Tenderness.

1. Among the few fellow-commoners in residence at Christ's College in the years 1710–24, of which Mr. J. A. Venn has kindly furnished me with a list, he thinks the one who best suits the above description to be Edward Finch, fifth son of the second Earl of Nottingham, who was admitted at Christ's in 1716, but migrated to Trinity in 1718. He afterwards became M.P. for the University.

2. Evidently John Baker, D.D., Fellow of Trinity and Vice-Master from 1722. See, as to his services, and subserviency, to the Master, the notice of him in *Dictionary of National Biography*, vol. iii (1885).

20.

Mr. S.,

I have just taken leave with my Sister and the good Company that came along with her; I had no Opportunity of going down with 'em or should gladly have embract it, for I shall be forc'd perhaps to go down by myself the next I can light on. We dined at my Ch^r, my Sister and I together, and talkt over all our Friends. I beg of you to speak to Mr. Ward if he has got my Measure for a Coat for I shall want one of same Colour with this last. Drugget for summer for this is a little worn out, should be obliged if you will speak to him first Opportunity that I may have it at Manc. I am told this Minute from Walker that Dr. Bentley & Dr. Whitfield[1] go to London in a Week or 10 days at furthest, Walker says he thinks to go with 'em, and if I meet with no opportunity of going directly from hence 'tis likely I may come with 'em. Our Book has been received with Applaus amongst all our friends, and those of our Enemies that are not quite Stupid say 'tis smartly wrote, 'tis commonly Judged to be the Joint Product of Dr. Whitfield, Tom Bentley, Walker & my Brain, only my Part they say was to draw it all up and give it the diction it possesses. My Printer and Pub. are miserably out, there's no reasoning with 'em since they understood no better. Where the [2] should our Booksellers write for a thing Printed for a Sham name by Nobody[3]; besides, 'tis not worth their while to give 'emselves any great trouble about what they get so little, they are above it but if they had been sent as I directed they would have gone off and money P^d and more sent for in an Instant. I tho't I had done enough to make them know it was Propaga-

1. As to John Whitfield, D.D., fellow of Trinity and afterwards Rector of Dicklebrugh (Norfolk), see Monk, vol. ii, pp. 106-7, where he is described as having been attached to the Master by personal regard and friendship, and as having quitted his fellowship ' before he had sullied his character by any unworthy compliances with the humour or schemes of his principal.'

2. A word (what could it have been ?) is obliterated here.

3. Cf. *ante*, p. 53; and *introductory remarks*.

M

tion[1] & not gain that was intended by't, tho' they took the right way to spoil both. I know several at this time that have said they want the Book and would buy it but cant get it, and the Booksellers to be sure are indifferent enough after the first Talks over. Have you sent by Bro. One? or any to Manchester or to Wakefield?[2] We lost our Opportunity to Tom. B. so that I an't sure that he has one yet. Snigs![3] Why doesn't he send 'em about. The Antidote wont spread so far as the Poison, send 'em, dispatch 'em, 50 to the Pole 40 to the Tzar 100 to Paris 3 to Vienna 80 to Leipsick[4] &c. I wish you would take into your own keeping 30 or 40 for my future Occasions. I wish you would write me word, how you do & your Wife & your Son, whose health I dont care if you assure me of next Post, tho' I wont expect it, I'm resolved, for I may be baulkt as I was last Post when the failure of an expected letter made me miss my sisters company all yesterday from One till 8. You are the most trusty Squire that I ever had, but not enough extravagant in the Point of Punctuality.

Coz Clowes[5] is chose Scholar 7 or 8 lads some his Seniors some Juniors turned out, the Mr gave me a very good Character of him.   T. B.

Rec[d] this Momt a Letter from Cos. Ann,[6] but have not time to answer.
ffarewell.

1. Or, as we should say, propaganda.
2. To Wakefield, because of the vicinity of Woodlesford. Cf. *ante*, p. 174 *note* 2.
3. '*Snigs.*' A popular oath.

Snigs, another.

A very perilous head, a dangerous brain.

Cartwright's *Ordinary* (1651).

Nares's *Glossary* (edd. Halliwell and Wright), vol. ii, p. 812.
4. As a great book-mart.
5. Joseph Clowes, cf. *ante*, p. 171 *note* 2; and p. 184 below.
6. Ann Byrom, daughter of Joseph Byrom. Cf. *Remains*, vol. i, p. 43 (where she announces to Stansfield John Byrom's marriage to her sister Elizabeth) *et al.*

II.

LETTERS FROM FRANCIS HOOPER TO JOHN BYROM, 1716—1726.

[The following letters addressed to John Byrom were copied from the originals, several years ago, by Mr. Hanby, the house-governor of the Chetham Hospital, who kindly gave them to Mr. Bailey. They fill up some *lacunae* in the Correspondence of John Byrom, and had they been forthcoming at the time, they would have found a place in his *Literary Remains*.

Francis Hooper, the writer of the letters, is called by Byrom "Father Francis," "Frank Hooper," and "my tutor." He was the son of John Hooper of Manchester and Catherine Mosley (*Mosley Family Memoirs*, p. 34). Like John Byrom, he was a member of Trinity College, Cambridge, under Bentley's Mastership. Hooper graduated as B.A. in 1716, and M.A. in 1720, and became a Fellow of the College. On January 22, 1719, he succeeded James Leicester, M.A. (who had held the office since August, 1712) as Library-Keeper of the Chetham Library, was chaplain to Lady Bland, the leader of the Manchester "assemblies," and was Incumbent of Didsbury, January 1721-2 to 1726. On the occasion of the visit of George II to the University of Cambridge in April 1728, the degree of D.D. was bestowed on Hooper— one of 286 persons on whom distinctions were conferred on that occasion. In 1739 he signed the recommendation of Byrom's Shorthand proposals. At his death in 1763 he was senior Dean and Senior of his College and left an estate to provide prizes (three silver goblets) for orations on subjects relating to the English nation. The following letters supply some other interesting details of his life. He was much in Byrom's company when in London, and their friendship was almost brotherly.

The first of the two following letters falls into place in Byrom's *Literary Remains* at page 32 of vol. i. It was written when Byrom, for private reasons of his own, had gone out of residence and betaken himself to Montpelier

(April, 1716), leaving his friends at home anxious about his welfare. Byrom graduated as B.A. in 1711, and as M.A. in 1715. In 1714 he had become a Fellow of his College (Trinity). In August, 1717, there was a dividend due to him, and the absent Byrom was told that Dr. Ashenhurst had promised to get what money he could, but that Mr. Baker (John Byrom's College tutor, as to whom cf. *ante*, p. 43) had refused paying anything without a receipt under John Byrom's hand. "Dr. Ashenhurst says there will be £50 due to you" (see *Remains*, vol. i, p. 35). Ward Grey Ashenhurst of Trinity College (B.A. 1704, M.A. 1708, M.D. 1715) was a physician who practised in the University; and it is said that, though he took the oaths of fealty to the house of Hanover, he would never accept a fee from a non-juror. The same oaths kept Byrom from returning to the University to take the Moderator's place in the nomination of his College. As to the terse and vigorous address to George I, then in Hanover, see Monk's *Life of Bentley*, vol. i, pp. 417 *sqq.*, where it is printed at length. Hooper's first letter, it will be noticed, states that the address was composed by Bentley himself. It was presented to Frederick Prince of Wales at Hampton Court by Dr. Daniel Waterland, Master of Magdalen, the Vice-Chancellor, attended by the heads of the University, introduced by Viscount Townshend, chief Secretary of State. Townshend was at the time befriending Bentley, whom he wished to employ in preparing a series of 'Friderician' editions to rival the Delphin Classics.[1] The "Commotions" at Trinity College relate to the renewal of the disputes which characterised the Master's rule, the first

---

1. Cf. Monk, vol. i, pp. 406-8. The series was intended to be *in usum Principis Frederici*, who was then eleven years old. The negotiation, said to have been suggested to Townshend by Chief Justices Parker and King, was, however, broken off—whether because the *honorarium* could not be settled to the intending editor's satisfaction, or because of Townshend's own eclipse, must be left undecided.

stage of which had come to an end in 1714 with the great trial in the hall of Ely house.   Edmund Miller, a fellow of Trinity College, and one of the leading antagonists of Dr. Bentley, was sergeant-at-law and Deputy High Steward of the University.   Bentley contrived to bring about his resignation of his fellowship, and got him dismissed from the Deputy High Stewardship.   Hooper's anticipation that this step had ended the quarrel was falsified.   In the following January, Miller wrote a book on the State of the University in general and Trinity College in particular, in consequence of which, "the whole University was put in commotion, and every dutiful son of Granta felt himself personally insulted."

In Byrom's *Remains* an interval occurs in his correspondence between July 17th, 1718, when he was in London, and April 17th, 1721, three months after his marriage. Early in 1718, his sister Phebe had written him that Mr. Lesley (as he or she called James Leicester) the Library-Keeper was going to die, and the Feoffees had asked if Byrom would have the place.   He replied he "could like it very well." (*Remains*, vol. i, p. 39.)   From Trinity College, on 3rd May following he wrote to his brother to say he would be very willing to have the Library, which was better worth while than staying at College for a doubtful chance for a fellowship; "besides 'tis in Manchester, which place I love entirely." (*Ib.*, p. 41.)   The librarianship, however, passed into the hands of the Rev. Francis Hooper, B.A., who was elected in 1718-19.   Soon after his election he wrote the following letter from Chetham's College.   "Clayton" mentioned therein is the Rev. John Clayton.[1]   There was another skeleton among the curiosities of the Library; for Byrom writing to his brother from Montpelier in 1718, and alluding to the Library, says, "I shall be glad to visit the skeleton."   In 1725 we find Byrom manifesting a curiosity to see the carcase of Jonathan Wild dissected at Surgeon's Hall],

1. Cf. *ante*, pp. 110 *sq*.

1.

Trin : Coll : Nobr. 1, 1716.

Mr. Byrom,

Doctor Ashenhurst[1] desires me to acquaint you, that he shou'd receive no small satisfaction in hearing of your wellfare. He has been very sollicitous with me to write to you and inform you that there is a dividend due; your part of which you may receive from him, as soon as ever he has your Orders to send it. He expresses some concern that he has not receiv'd your answers to his letters, & hopes you'll remove that uneasiness by writing either to him or me the first opportunity.

We expected here that you wou'd have come to have accepted the Moderators place[2]; but if we may judg by the consequences of things, it wou'd only have put you to the inconvenience of a journey without meeting with any success, the same *it interest* you wou'd have had being the reason of Whitton's[3] losing it, the University thinking it a breach of the Proctors Priviledge to have (as they called it) a Moderator impos'd upon him without his own free consent and Determination.

We have lately presented a very loyall address to be sent to the King at Hanover; it was drawn up by Doctor Bentley, who is still at London, & sumptuously entertained ev'ry day

1. Clearly W. Grey Ashenhurst of Trinity. (See *introductory note*.)

2. The *Moderatores in Scholis publicis Sophistorum et Baccalancorum* were appointed annually by Grace of the Senate, as they still are under that name for the Mathematical Tripos, on the nomination of the several colleges in rotation. The claim of the Senior Proctor.

3. John Whitton, Trin. Coll., B.A. 1712, M.A. 1716 (J. E. B.).

by my Lord Townsend.[1] His [Bentley's] interest begins to be very strong at Court, & its thought He will be made sensible of it the first opportunity they have to preffer him. There have been great commotions in College since you have been absent from it, our old divisions having been again renew'd; but I believe they are now ended, since Mr. Miller, who was generally the cause of them, is deserted by all the fellows, who by depriving him of the privilege of voting, have put it out of his power to do any further mischief.[2] I don't know of anything that has happen'd else that is materiall, & shou'd not have given you the trouble of this letter only to have inform'd you, what probably you had heard before, were it not the request of your friend the Doctor, which I hope will excuse for

Yours to command

FRAN: HOOPER.

Pray present my Services to all friends.

2.

[Manchester] Coll: Ap. the 20, 1719.

Monsr. Byrom,

I had the satisfaction of a letter from your C. Allen's [3] man & the pleasure to hear by him that you are all well: I wish to

1. On the suppression of the Rebellion of 1715, an address of congratulation to the King, from the Senate of the University of Cambridge, was drawn up by Bentley; but, two members of the *Caput* having vetoed the proposed grace for sealing and presenting it, the address had to be deferred. Bentley, however, having assured the Secretary of State, Viscount Townshend, that the address should be put through, contrived by an ingeniously devised surprise to carry it on October 16th 1716, and immediately posted to town with the Vice-Chancellor, Dr. Waterland, for its presentation. For a full account of this extraordinary *tour de force*, see Monk, vol. i, pp. 4, 7, 422, where the address itself is given at length.

2. As to the 'commotions in College' in September and October 1716, see *ib.*, pp. 408 *sqq.* The Master and seven Fellows, in the absence of Colbatch, Bentley's chief opponent, subscribed an Order, that Miller (and another) should not be allowed to act as Fellows.

3. Cf. *ante*, p. 168, *note* 3, as to 'Cousin Allen.'

be amongst you heartily, but cannot come immediately without disoblidging those persons who very industrious in
bringing me into this place.   The library before now has not
been open'd for some time, that[1] it is become a novelty, &
frequented by a great many, I believe, only upon that
account.   I have pretty good opportunity's of reading here,
& hope I shall now be master of a good deal of time, so that I
shall endeavour to qualifie myself, as well as I can, against
the great the important day.   Our Audit here is upon the 14th
of May, when we shall have a full meeting of the Governours
for the making up of the Coll : Accounts &, its thought, an
Order for the buying of some books into the Library : Mr.
Leicester's long illness obliged him to omitt that part of his
office, so that we have 300 p. in bank for that purpose.

I had much satisfaction in being inform'd by your sister of
our Country man's[2] success at Scholarships, & that his private
conversation with Dr. Bentley may make him hope for future
encouragement from that great man.   I am glad to hear that
his cause go's on so successfully, & that the further they
search into the merits of it it still gains a new lustre.   I have
rec[d] abundance of pleasure from the perusall of the review,[3]
which by a fortunate accident fell into my hands, it discovers
a great deal of bravery, & shews (which is very rare in
controversy's of this nature, when the University has had so
many Woddy's[4] to take the wrong side) that the author is
bold enough to speak the truth : its pitty that the Drs. Court
friends[5] are so long a coming, or that justice & right shou'd

1. So that.

2. *i.e.*, the man from our county's.   The reference seems to be to
young Clowes, *ante*, p. 178.

3. Byrom's pamphlet so called.

4. *Woddy* seems to be a diminution of wood (M.E. wod)=mad,
furious. See Skeat's *Etymological Dictionary of the English
Language*, s.v. wood.

5. The Whig Government, and the Chancellor Lord Parker in
particular.   Whatever might have been the effect of a royal commission, the delay as to Trinity College matters was to Bentley's
advantage. Cf. Monk, vol. ii, p. 83.

be forced to the necessity of flying there for protection and succour.

Little Medium[1] do's not, I fancy, intend to oblige us this bout. He cou'd never have done it more opportunely, or in a more convenient place than Chappel, from whence his soul might have took its flight an offering fit for Heaven; tho' I think by the No of vacancies, & prospects we have, our year[2] has no great reason to complain. I believe it will be towards Septr before I can make my appearance; but have reason to hope, since absence has been excused to so many upon such like occasions, that it will be no objection against me.

We were in hopes of seeing you here the last week, some of us had propos'd to have given you the meeting at Buxton upon Thursday, if Mr. Clowes & your Sister had not arriv'd the day before, & put an end to our expectations. I believe, & cannot say but I wish that I may find you in Coll: when I come up; for we may presume, if *Non Omnino*[3] was the Author of the late elegant pamphlet, that the Dr. is much in his debt, & cannot refuse a favour to him who has been so serviceable, hearty, & successful in his Cause.

Clayton sends his service to you. When we are all together, He intends to cut up a Body for us, & present the Skeleton[4] to the Library. Your Brother [Edward Byrom] is very

1. *Little Medium* (not 'little Premium') may conceivably be Mr. Miller, whose resignation of his fellowship was already in the wind; or is the profanity more outrageous?

2. Hooper took his B.A. in 1716; Byrom in 1711.

3. See *introductory remarks*.

4. According to Mr. Albert Nicholson, in his pleasant little book, *The Chetham Hospital and Library* (1910), pp. 86-7, a strangely various collection of curiosities had been from time to time deposited in the Chetham Library, till about fifty years ago they were handed over to the Peel Park Museum. At the Library they were exhibited to visitors by a Chetham schoolboy: " That's the skeleton of a mon—that's a globe—that's a telescope—that's a snake," etc. Dr. Axon informs me that a pamphlet reproduction of this remarkable monologue was printed in 1828 by John Stanley Gregson.

curious that way, whom I expected here this morning to have drunk your health in a dish of tea; but on account of his not coming, & post's going out, can but give you an imperfect account of what you requested in one of your letters to him viz. that you rec^d nine pounds for the income of your room the Value of the Bed He cannot guess at, most of the Stuff being your own when it was made up, pray give my service to all friends, & be so kind to write to me as often as you can spare time which favours shall be acknowledged by Your H.S.

F. HOOPER.

To Mr. JOHN BYROM
    att Trinity College
        In Cambridge.

APPENDIX II.

ADDENDA ET CORRIGENDA to Vols. I and II.

VOL. I.

Page 5. *A Pastoral.* Add to *introductory note* :

These stanzas were parodied by Crabbe in his early days. See *Life* by his son (*Works*, vol. i, 1834), where the first two stanzas quoted—and where the original is ascribed to Shenstone.

Page 218. Add to *introductory note* :

The *Poems* of the excellent ' Mrs.' Elizabeth Carter, which fill vol. ii. of the *Memoirs,* edited by the Rev. Montagu Pennington, 2nd ed., 1816, contain (pp. 24-6) some couplets *To Mr. Duck, occasioned by a present of his poems,* which, as the editor audaciously observes, seem to have been inspired by Mr. Duck's own Muse, and which she (the editor) would not have inserted, ' had they not been published before.'

Page 221, l. 8. The late Sir Leslie Stephen, who wrote the notice of Byrom in the *Dictionary of National Biography,* vol. viii (1886), and who, after the appearance of the first and second volumes of this edition, published a delightful article on Byrom in the *National Review,* vol. 27 (reprinted in his *Studies of a Biographer,* vol. i, 1898), wrote to me on March 6th, 1896 : " This gap should be filled, I guess, with ' *His Hessians.*' In Stanhope's *History of England,* vol. ii, p. 123, you will see that in 1728 Horace Walpole proposed to take 12,000 Hessians into British pay, which was carried—against all reason, as Stanhope thinks—by a large majority. ' Sir Harry ' is no doubt Sir Henry de Hoghton, Bart., M.P. for Preston, to whom Byrom applied on March 31st, 1731 (see *Remains,* vol. i, p. 454), about the Workhouse Bill. From the *Parliamentary History,* vol. viii, I see that Hoghton voted for Walpole in the only two lists given. This, I think, satisfies all the conditions."

Beyond doubt, it does ; and I am very glad to have an opportunity of citing the letter of an honoured friend, whose interest in Byrom gave me very great pleasure.

Page 368, *note*, l. 8 from bottom.

Weigelius. See the interesting account of this ' gentle mystic,' and of the *Outlines Anti-Weigelianae* by John Arrowsmith, Master of Trinity, inveighing against Weigel's depreciation of University teaching, in Dr. J. Bass Mullinger's *The University of Cambridge*, vol. iii (1911), pp. 477—481.

Page 436, *introductory note.*

As to Brown's *Estimate* see *Correspondence between Gray and Mason*, ed. J. Mitford, 1853, pp. 76 and 496.

Page 465, *introductory note* to stanzas *On the Patron of England.*

Cf. Sir Thomas Browne's *Enquiries into Vulgar Errors*, bk. vii, ch. xvi : *On the Picture of St. George.* Works, ed. S. Wilkin, 1835, vol. iii, pp. 138-40.

Page 477.   *Introductory Note* to *An Epistle to J. Bl-k-n, Esq.*

Cf. the same work, bk. vii, ch. ix : *On the Food of John Baptist, Locusts and Wild Honey; ib.*, vol. iii, pp. 319—321.

VOL. II.

Page 65, l. 17.   *For* Appendix II *read* Appendix V.

Page 172, *introductory note* on *Enthusiasm.*

By the side of Wesley's denunciation of ' enthusiasm ' should, however, be read the following passage from a letter addressed by him to the ' author ' (? editor) of *The Westminster Journal* and reproduced in his Journal, s.d., January 5th 1761 (edn. 1827, vol. iii, p. 34) :—

" Your correspondent is, doubtless, a man of sense; and he seems to write in a good humour. But he is extremely little acquainted with the persons of whom he undertakes to give an account.

' There is gone abroad,' says he, ' an ungoverned spirit of enthusiasm, propagated by knaves, and embraced by fools.' Suffer me now to address the gentleman himself. Sir, you may call me both a knave and a fool; but prove me either one or the other, if you can. ' Why, you are an enthusiast.' What do you mean by the term ?   A believer in Jesus Christ ?   An asserter of his equality with the Father, and of the entire Christian Revelation ?   Do you mean one who maintains the antiquated doctrines of the New Birth, and Justification of Faith? Then I am an enthusiast. But if you mean anything else, either prove or retract the charge.

" The enthusiasm which has lately gone abroad is faith which worketh by love. Does this ' endanger government itself? ' Just the reverse. Fearing God, it honours the King. It teaches all men to be subject to the higher powers; not for wrath, but for conscience sake."

Page 592 (Appendix), p. 591 and *note*.

Query, was the E. Lampe who signs the curious letter proposing to Byrom a disputation on Quakerism at Stockport, and to whom Byrom replies in a tone less charitable than was usual with him at any period of his life, Ephraim, son of Henry Lampe? The autobiography of the father (*Curriculum Vitæ, or The Birth, Education, Travels and Life of Henry Lamp, M.D., written by himself . . . in Ulverstone, in Fourness, in Lancashire, the 22nd day of the 1st Mo., 1710–11*) was published in 1895, with introduction and notes, by Joseph J. Green, and is a very curious record of an interesting man, born at Königsberg in 1660. He settled as a physician at Ulverston in 1698, and died in 1710, as a member of the Society of Friends, which he had joined at Canterbury some years previously. His elder son, Ephraim, is mentioned in his will, but is not heard of again, unless he was Byrom's combative acquaintance.

INDEX.

———